Publisher
Robyn Moore

Color
Brian Miller

abstractstudiocomics.com
mail@abstractstudiocomics.com

Terry Moore's ECHO: Black Hole published by Abstract Studio, Box 271487, Houston, Texas 77277-1487.

ECHO

BLACK HOLE

by
Terry Moore

"When a finger points to the moon,
the imbecile looks at the finger."
—Chinese proverb

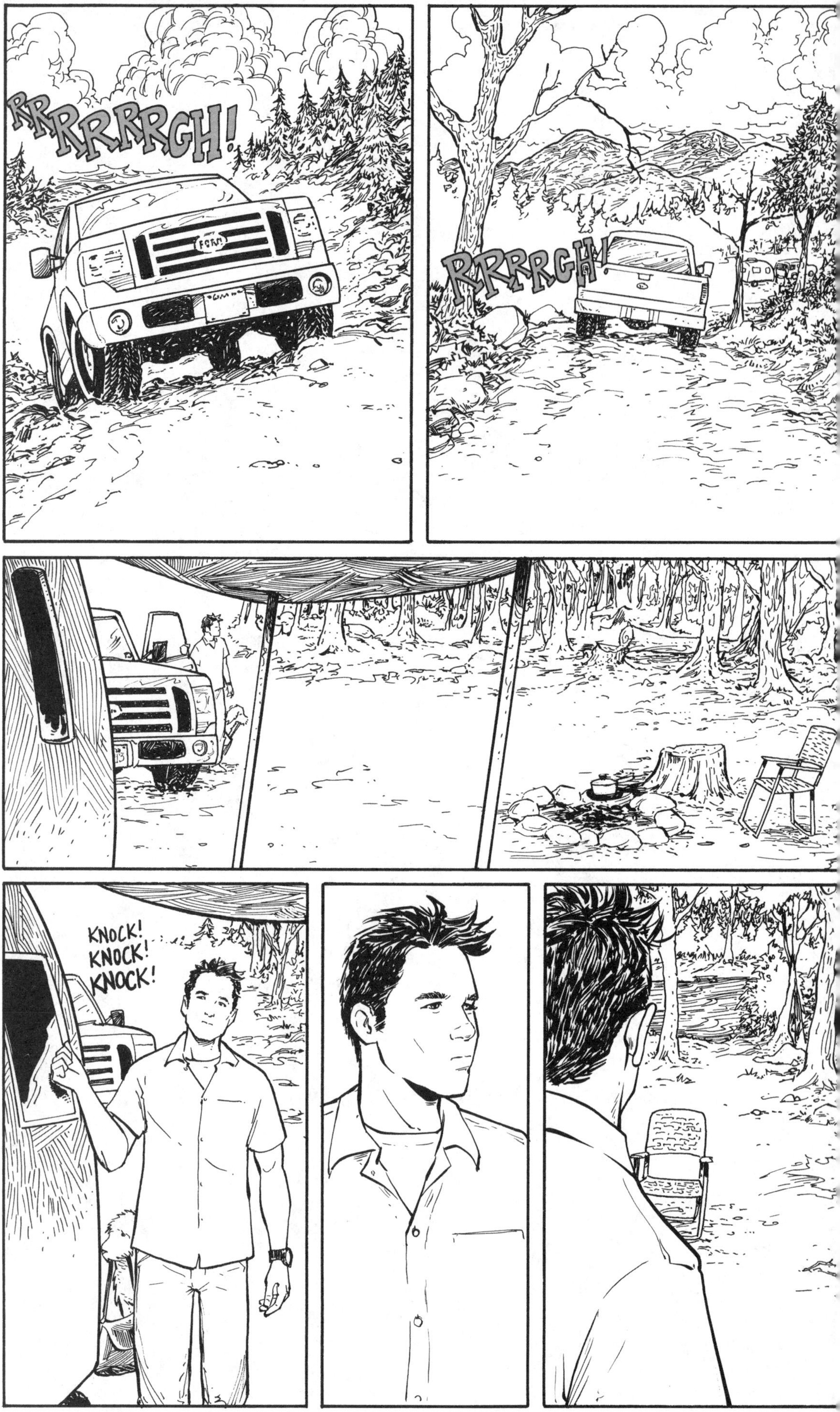
RRRRRRRGH!
RRRRRGH!
KNOCK! KNOCK! KNOCK!

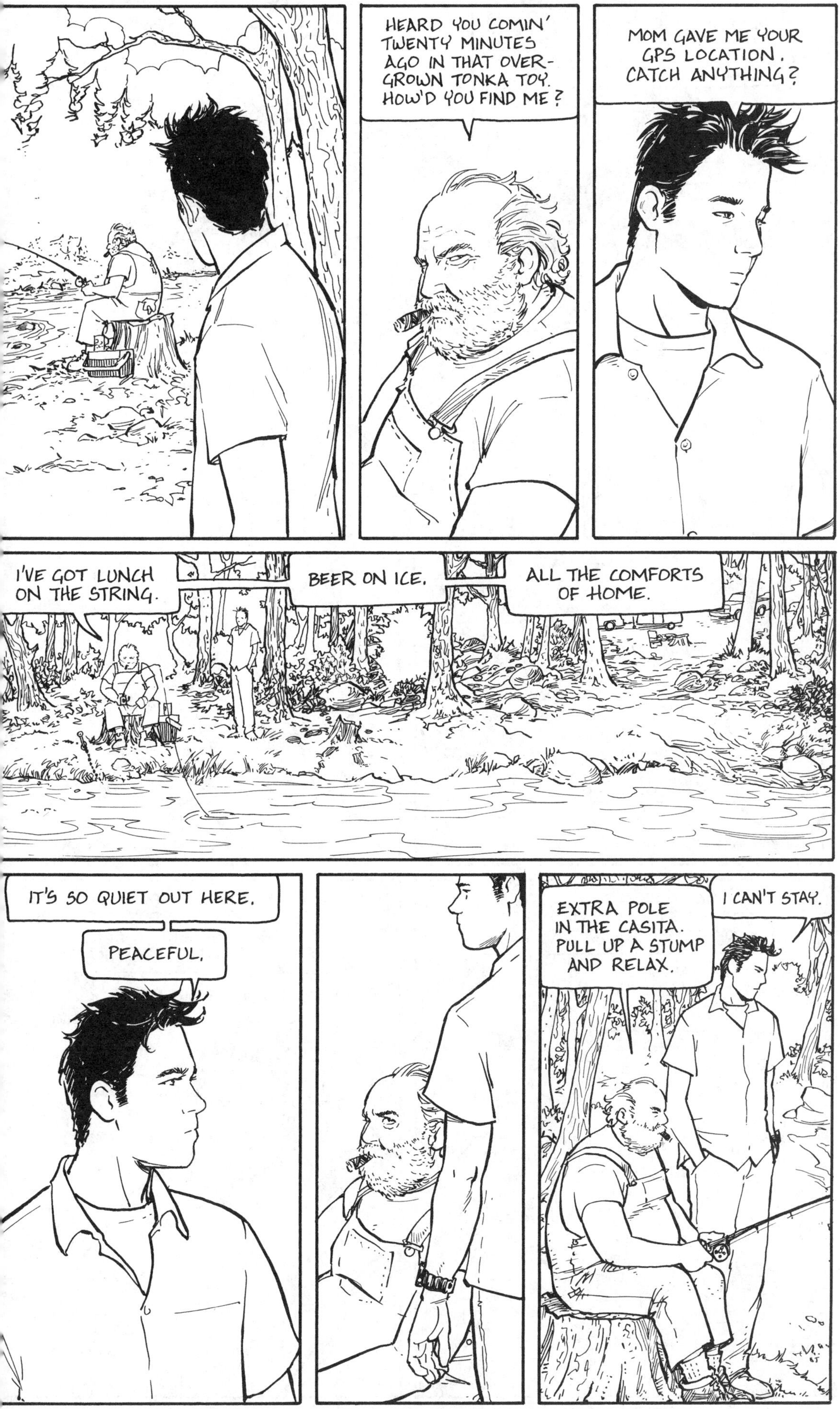
HEARD YOU COMIN' TWENTY MINUTES AGO IN THAT OVER-GROWN TONKA TOY. HOW'D YOU FIND ME?
MOM GAVE ME YOUR GPS LOCATION. CATCH ANYTHING?
I'VE GOT LUNCH ON THE STRING.
BEER ON ICE.
ALL THE COMFORTS OF HOME.
IT'S SO QUIET OUT HERE.
PEACEFUL.
EXTRA POLE IN THE CASITA. PULL UP A STUMP AND RELAX.
I CAN'T STAY.

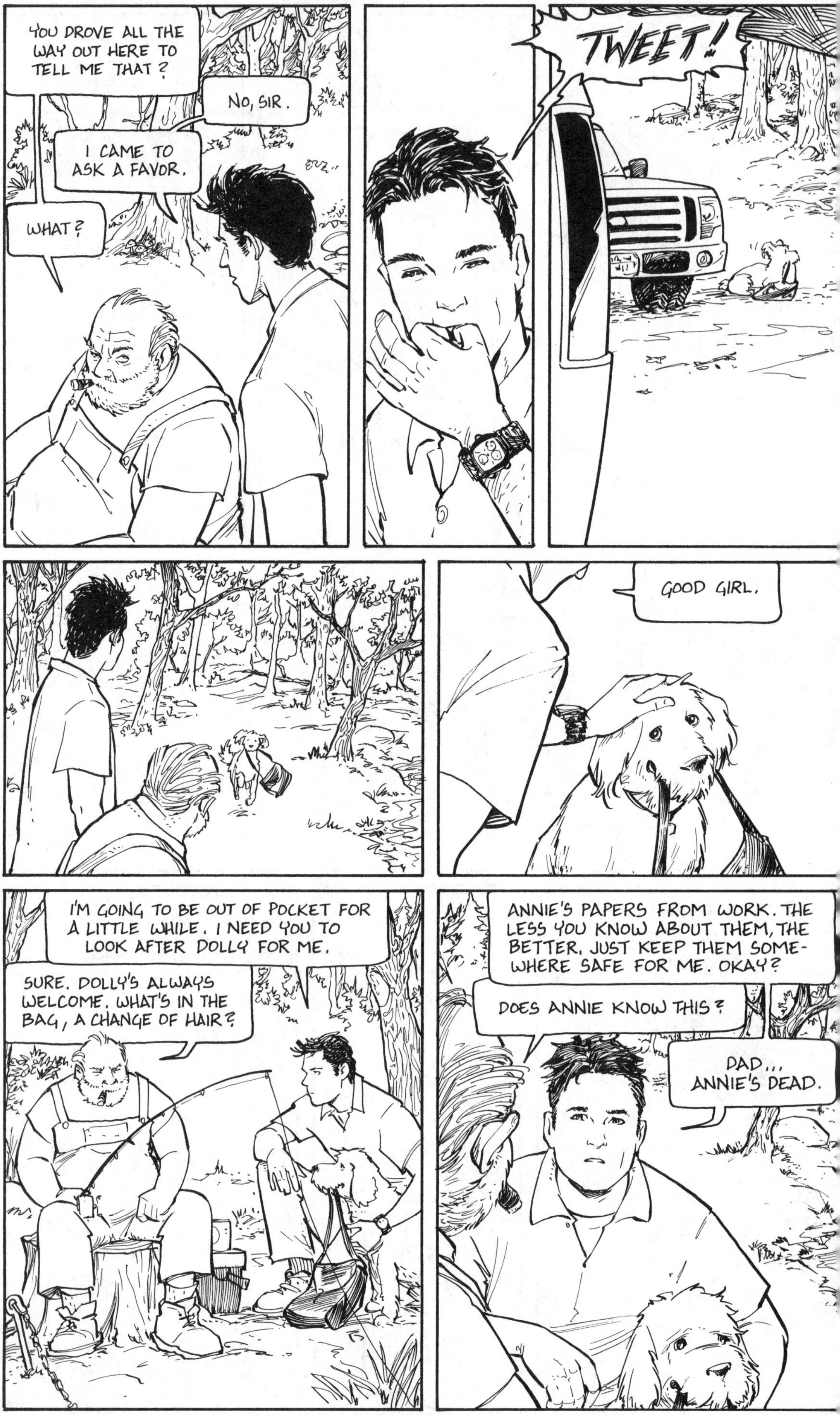
YOU DROVE ALL THE WAY OUT HERE TO TELL ME THAT?
NO, SIR.
I CAME TO ASK A FAVOR.
WHAT?
TWEET!
GOOD GIRL.
I'M GOING TO BE OUT OF POCKET FOR A LITTLE WHILE. I NEED YOU TO LOOK AFTER DOLLY FOR ME.
SURE. DOLLY'S ALWAYS WELCOME. WHAT'S IN THE BAG, A CHANGE OF HAIR?
ANNIE'S PAPERS FROM WORK. THE LESS YOU KNOW ABOUT THEM, THE BETTER. JUST KEEP THEM SOME-WHERE SAFE FOR ME. OKAY?
DOES ANNIE KNOW THIS?
DAD... ANNIE'S DEAD.

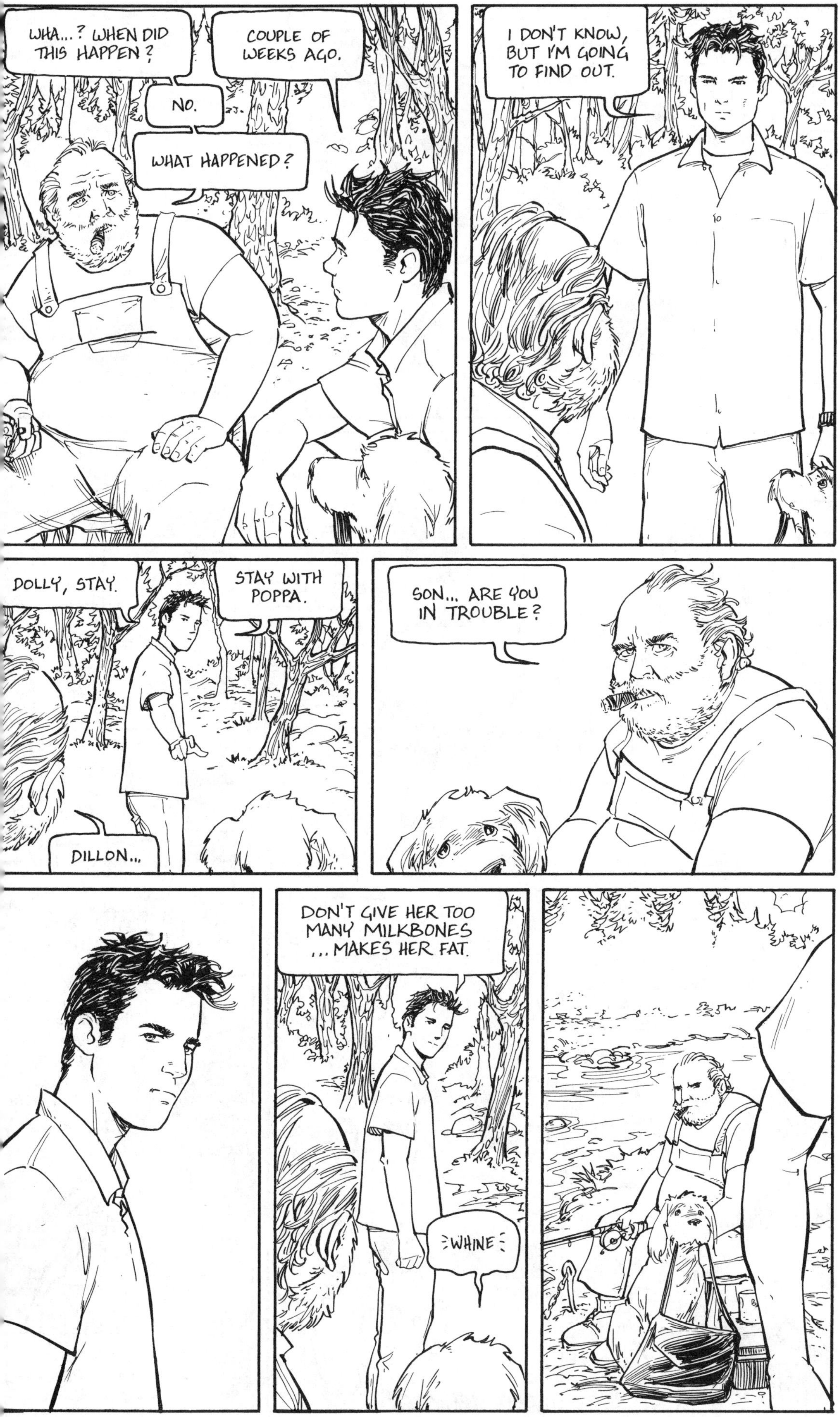
WHA...? WHEN DID THIS HAPPEN?
COUPLE OF WEEKS AGO.
NO.
WHAT HAPPENED?
I DON'T KNOW, BUT I'M GOING TO FIND OUT.
DOLLY, STAY.
STAY WITH POPPA.
DILLON...
SON... ARE YOU IN TROUBLE?
DON'T GIVE HER TOO MANY MILKBONES ...MAKES HER FAT.
WHINE

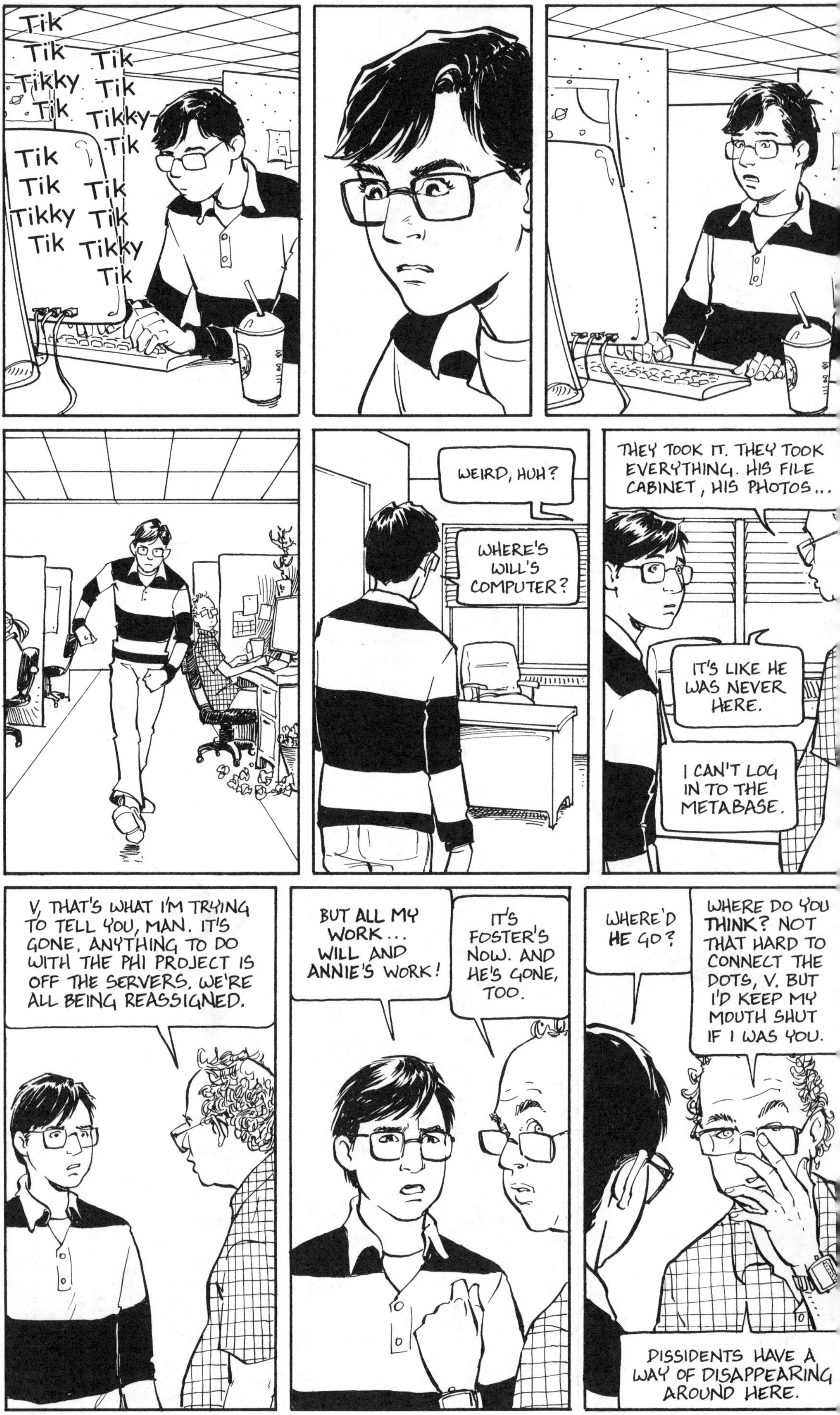
Tik
Tik
Tikky
Tik
Tik
Tik
Tikky
Tik
Tik
Tik
Tikky
Tik
Tik
Tik
Tik
Tikky
Tik
WEIRD, HUH?
WHERE'S WILL'S COMPUTER?
THEY TOOK IT. THEY TOOK EVERYTHING. HIS FILE CABINET, HIS PHOTOS...
IT'S LIKE HE WAS NEVER HERE.
I CAN'T LOG IN TO THE METABASE.
V, THAT'S WHAT I'M TRYING TO TELL YOU, MAN. IT'S GONE. ANYTHING TO DO WITH THE PHI PROJECT IS OFF THE SERVERS. WE'RE ALL BEING REASSIGNED.
BUT ALL MY WORK... WILL AND ANNIE'S WORK!
IT'S FOSTER'S NOW. AND HE'S GONE, TOO.
WHERE'D HE GO?
WHERE DO YOU THINK? NOT THAT HARD TO CONNECT THE DOTS, V. BUT I'D KEEP MY MOUTH SHUT IF I WAS YOU.
DISSIDENTS HAVE A WAY OF DISAPPEARING AROUND HERE.

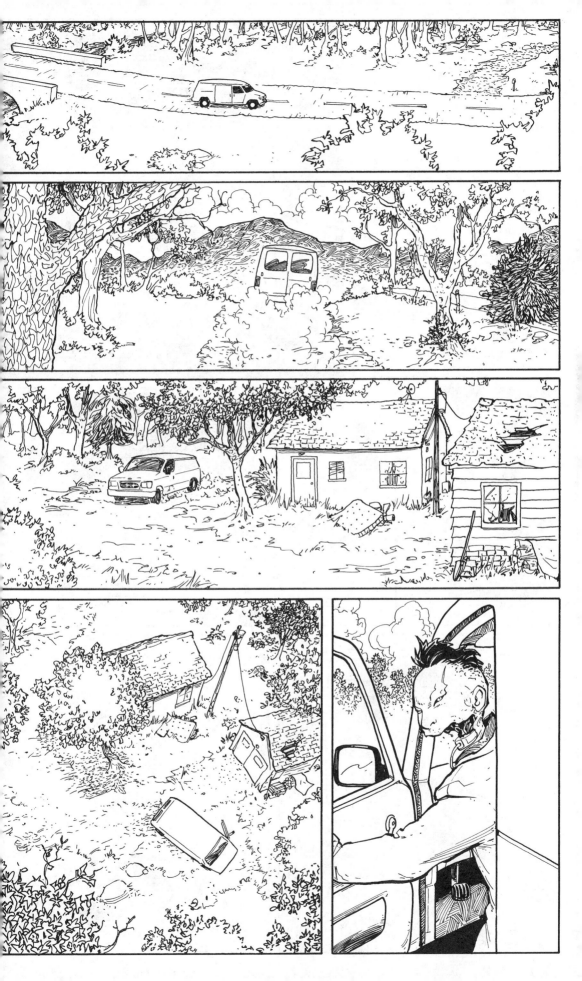

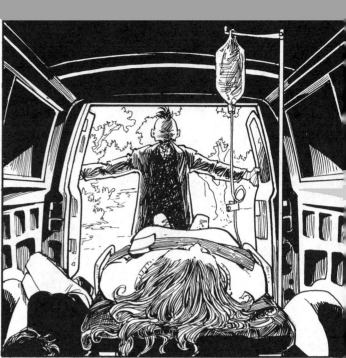

WHOOSH!

THUD!

SQUEAK!
SQUEAK!

SQUEEK

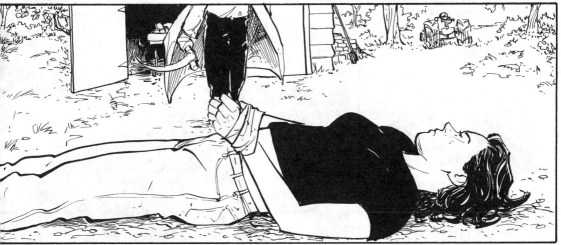

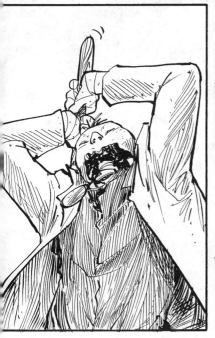

WHAAK!

SHRRRGH!
SHRRRGH!

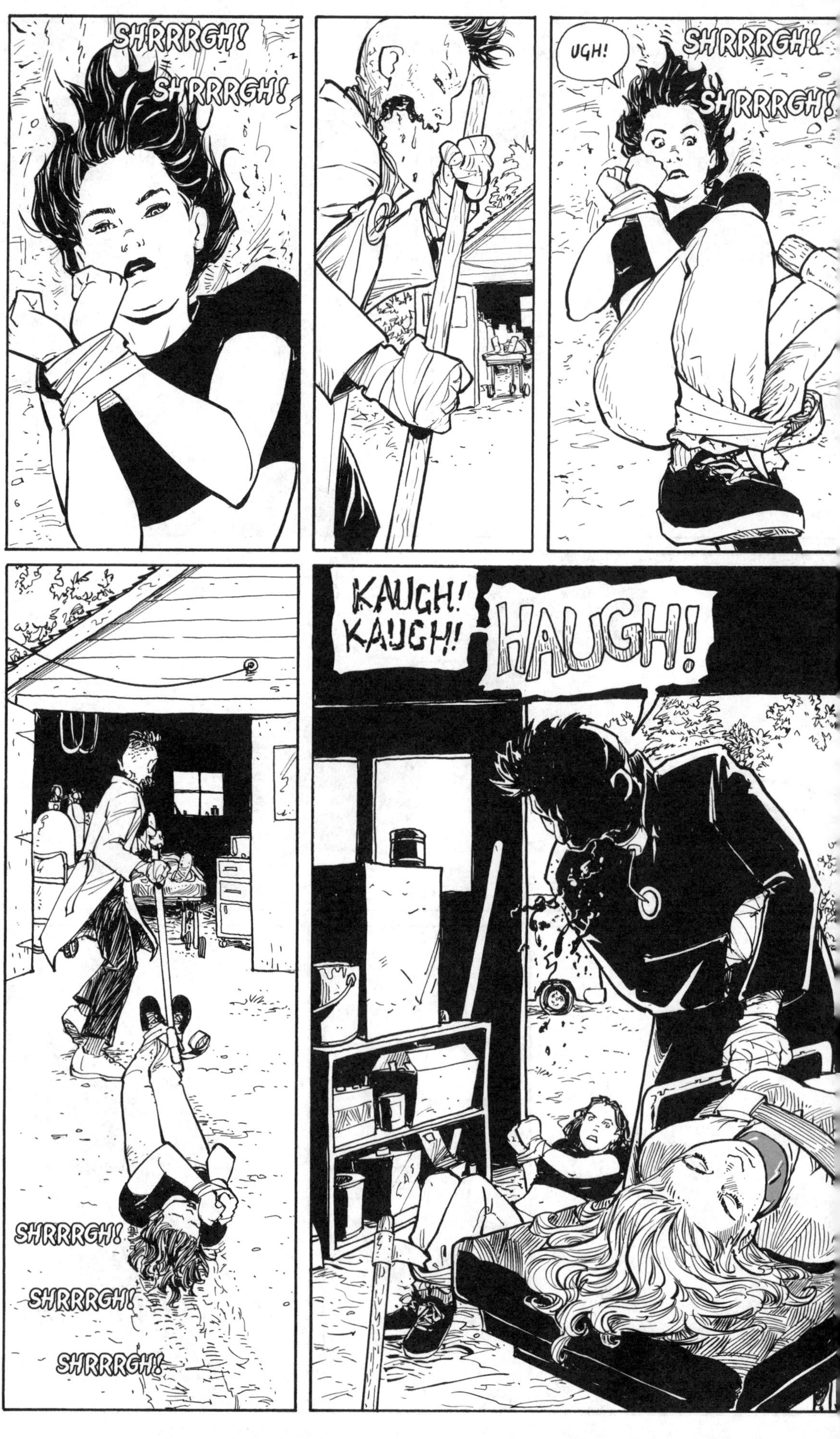
SHRRRGH!
SHRRRGH!
UGH!
SHRRRGH!
SHRRRGH!
SHRRRGH!
SHRRRGH!
SHRRRGH!
KAUGH! KAUGH!
HAUGH!

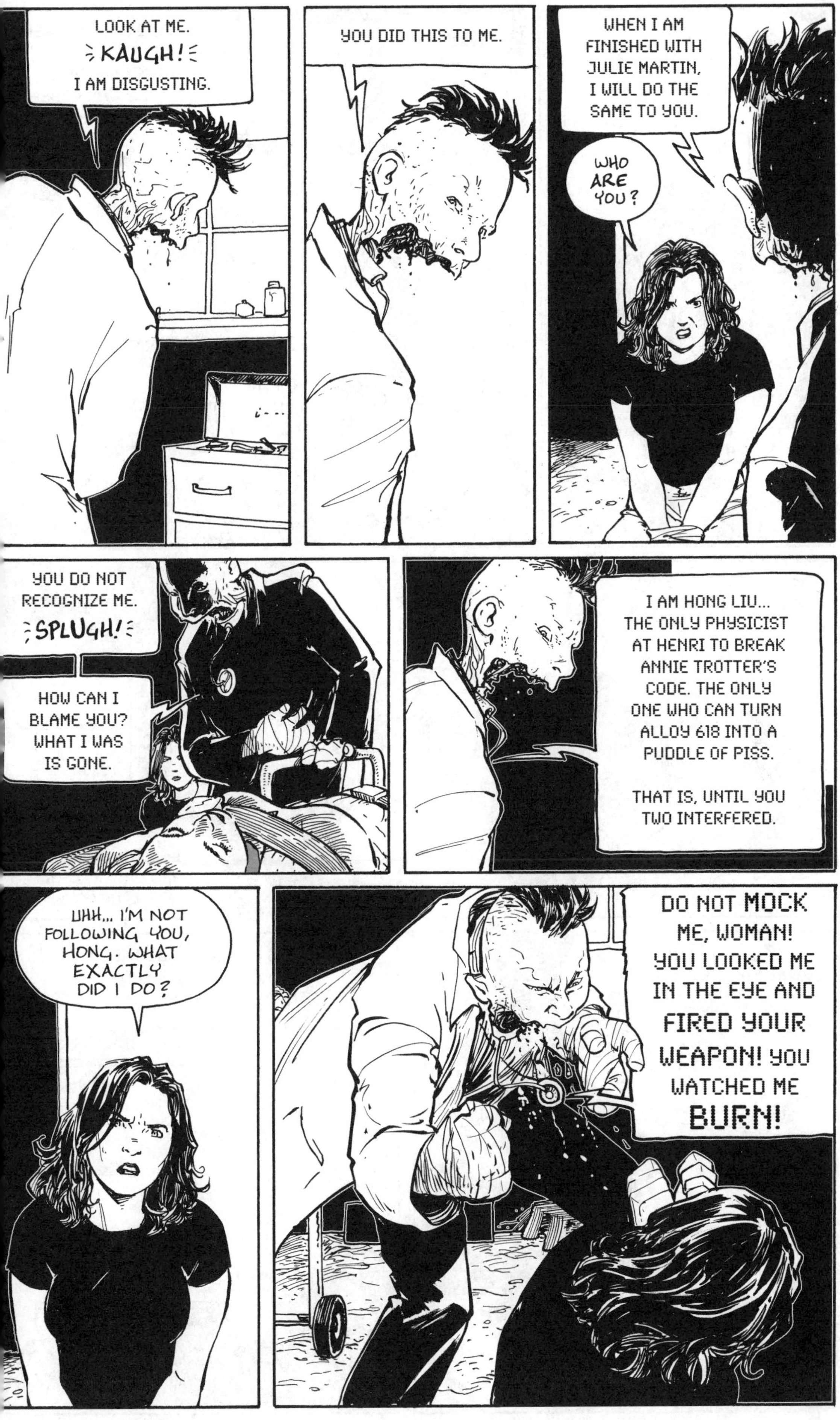
LOOK AT ME.
KAUGH!
I AM DISGUSTING.
YOU DID THIS TO ME.
WHEN I AM FINISHED WITH JULIE MARTIN, I WILL DO THE SAME TO YOU.
WHO ARE YOU?
YOU DO NOT RECOGNIZE ME.
SPLUGH!
HOW CAN I BLAME YOU? WHAT I WAS IS GONE.
I AM HONG LIU... THE ONLY PHYSICIST AT HENRI TO BREAK ANNIE TROTTER'S CODE. THE ONLY ONE WHO CAN TURN ALLOY 618 INTO A PUDDLE OF PISS.
THAT IS, UNTIL YOU TWO INTERFERED.
UHH... I'M NOT FOLLOWING YOU, HONG. WHAT EXACTLY DID I DO?
DO NOT MOCK ME, WOMAN! YOU LOOKED ME IN THE EYE AND FIRED YOUR WEAPON! YOU WATCHED ME BURN!

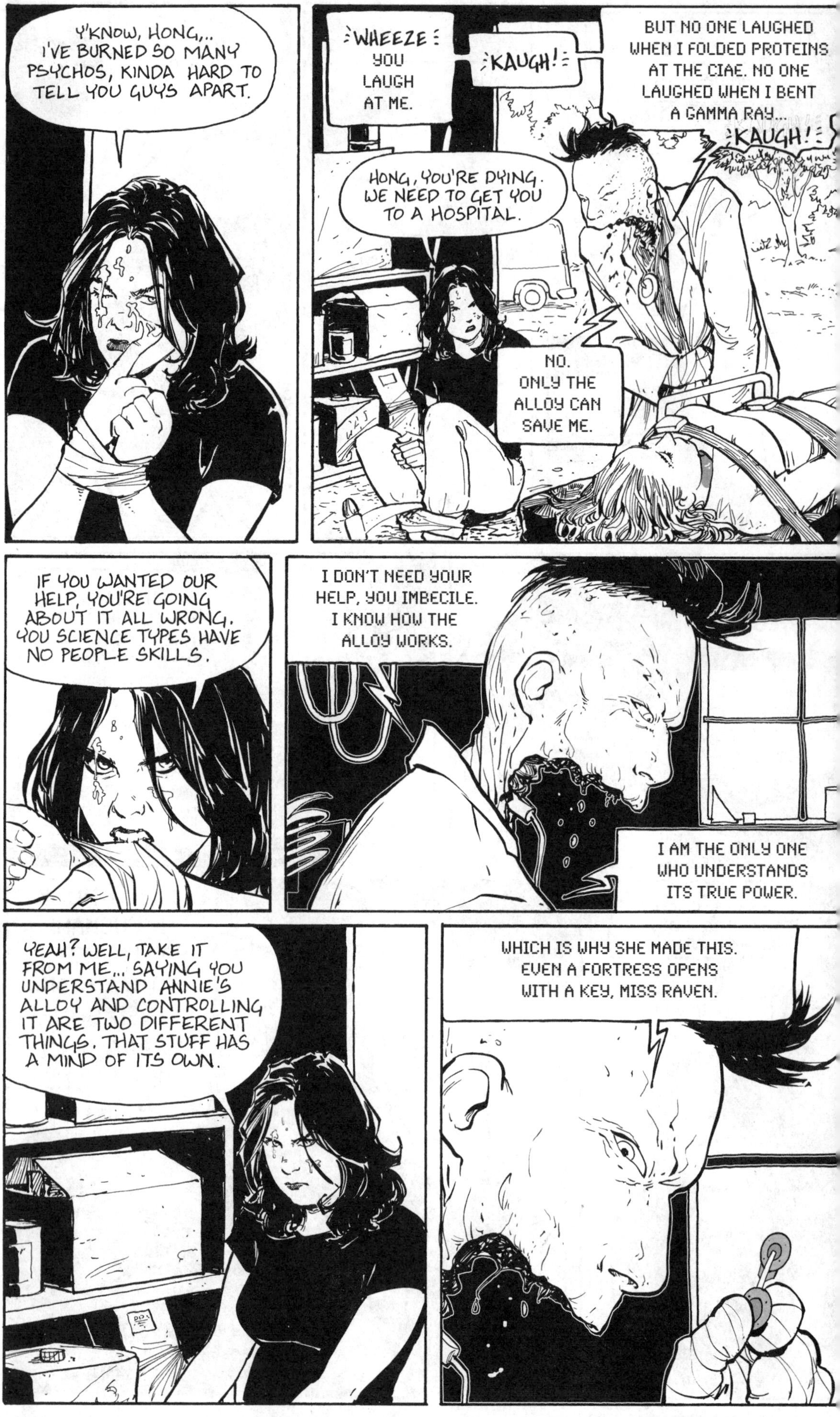
Y'KNOW, HONG,.. I'VE BURNED SO MANY PSYCHOS, KINDA HARD TO TELL YOU GUYS APART.
WHEEZE
YOU LAUGH AT ME.
KAUGH!
BUT NO ONE LAUGHED WHEN I FOLDED PROTEINS AT THE CIAE. NO ONE LAUGHED WHEN I BENT A GAMMA RAY...
KAUGH!
HONG, YOU'RE DYING. WE NEED TO GET YOU TO A HOSPITAL.
NO. ONLY THE ALLOY CAN SAVE ME.
IF YOU WANTED OUR HELP, YOU'RE GOING ABOUT IT ALL WRONG. YOU SCIENCE TYPES HAVE NO PEOPLE SKILLS.
I DON'T NEED YOUR HELP, YOU IMBECILE. I KNOW HOW THE ALLOY WORKS.
I AM THE ONLY ONE WHO UNDERSTANDS ITS TRUE POWER.
YEAH? WELL, TAKE IT FROM ME... SAYING YOU UNDERSTAND ANNIE'S ALLOY AND CONTROLLING IT ARE TWO DIFFERENT THINGS. THAT STUFF HAS A MIND OF ITS OWN.
WHICH IS WHY SHE MADE THIS. EVEN A FORTRESS OPENS WITH A KEY, MISS RAVEN.

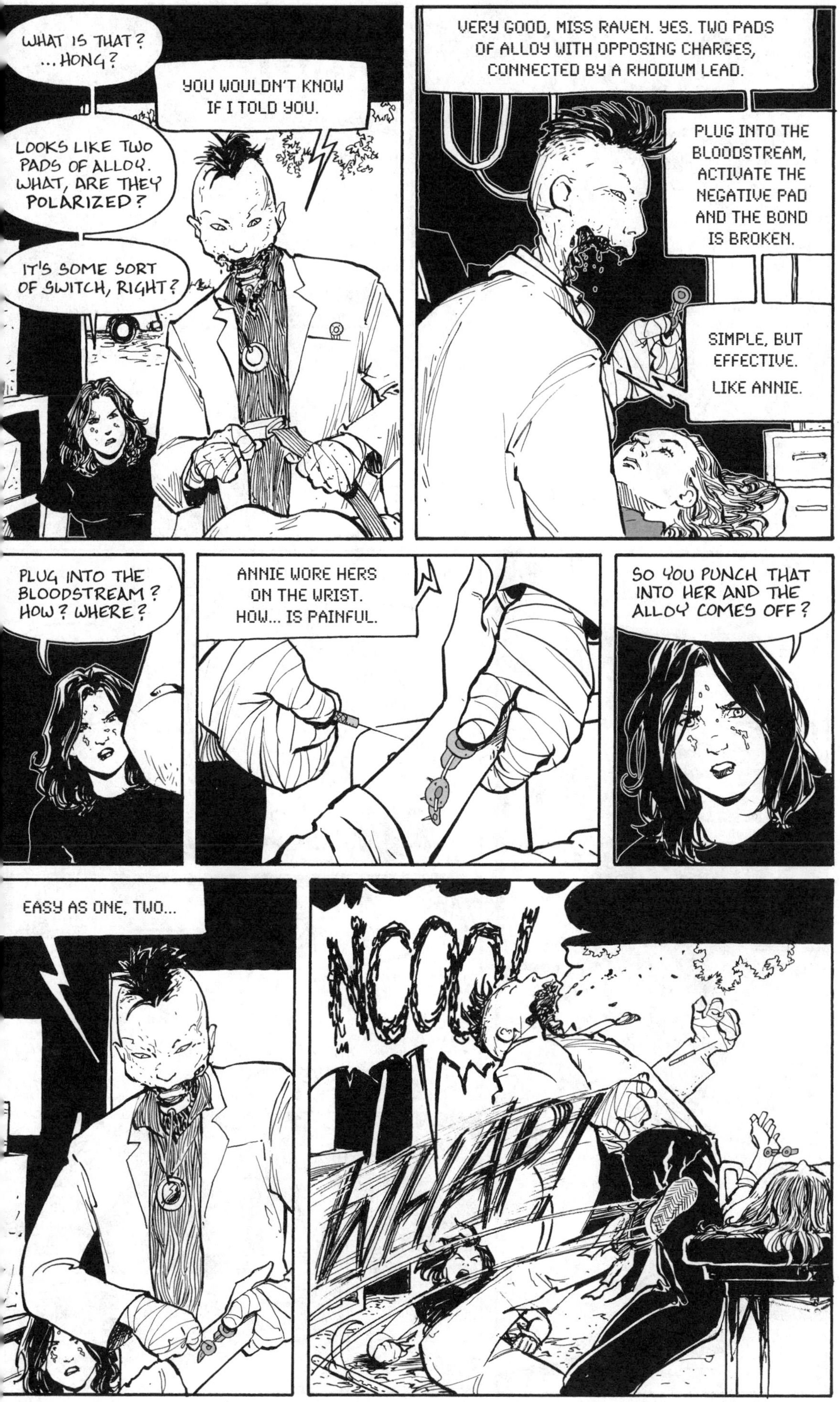
WHAT IS THAT? ...HONG?
YOU WOULDN'T KNOW IF I TOLD YOU.
LOOKS LIKE TWO PADS OF ALLOY. WHAT, ARE THEY POLARIZED?
IT'S SOME SORT OF SWITCH, RIGHT?
VERY GOOD, MISS RAVEN. YES. TWO PADS OF ALLOY WITH OPPOSING CHARGES, CONNECTED BY A RHODIUM LEAD.
PLUG INTO THE BLOODSTREAM, ACTIVATE THE NEGATIVE PAD AND THE BOND IS BROKEN.
SIMPLE, BUT EFFECTIVE.
LIKE ANNIE.
PLUG INTO THE BLOODSTREAM? HOW? WHERE?
ANNIE WORE HERS ON THE WRIST. HOW... IS PAINFUL.
SO YOU PUNCH THAT INTO HER AND THE ALLOY COMES OFF?
EASY AS ONE, TWO...
NOOO!
WHAP!

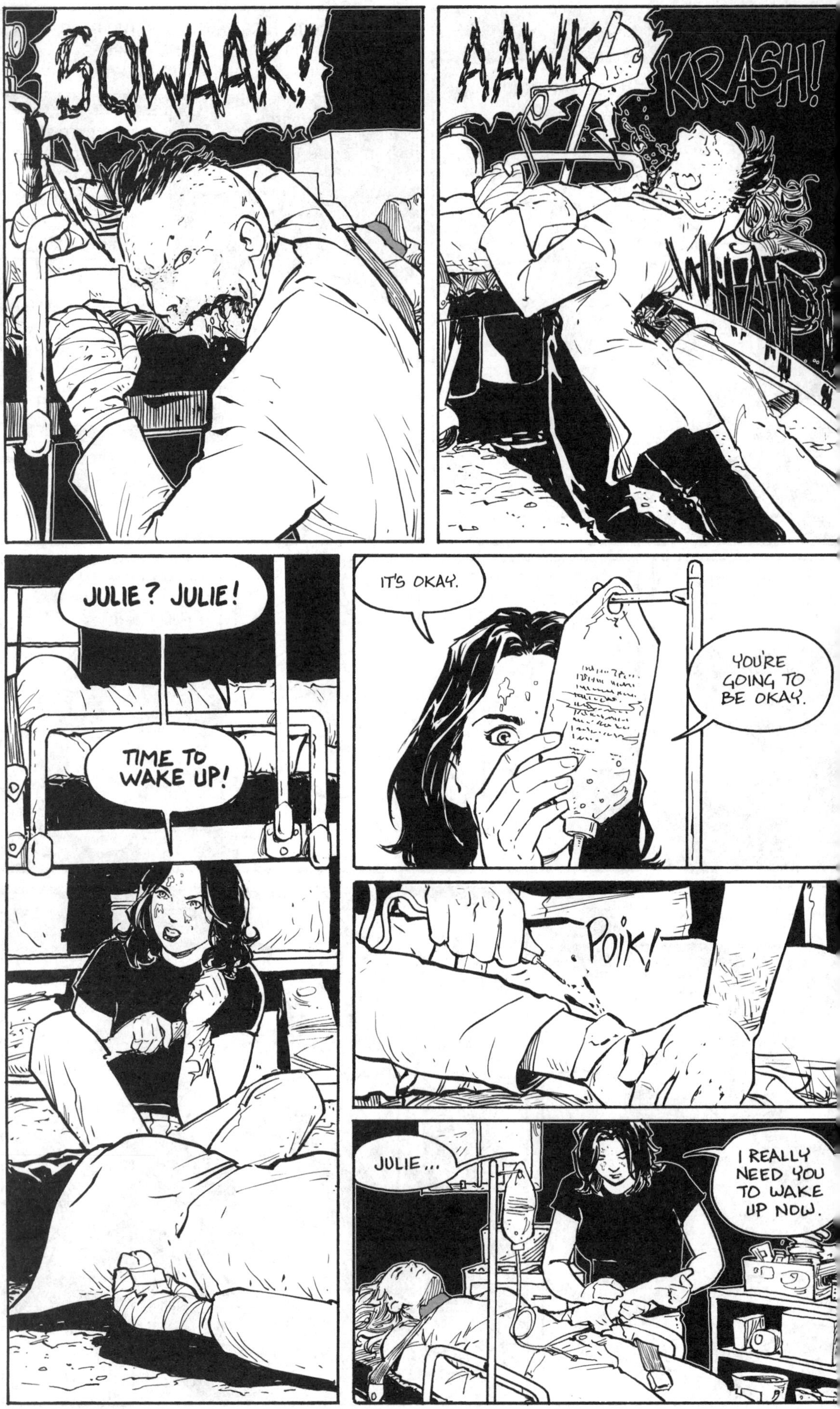
SQWAAK!
AAWK!
KRASH!
WHAP!
JULIE? JULIE!
TIME TO WAKE UP!
IT'S OKAY.
YOU'RE GOING TO BE OKAY.
POIK!
JULIE...
I REALLY NEED YOU TO WAKE UP NOW.

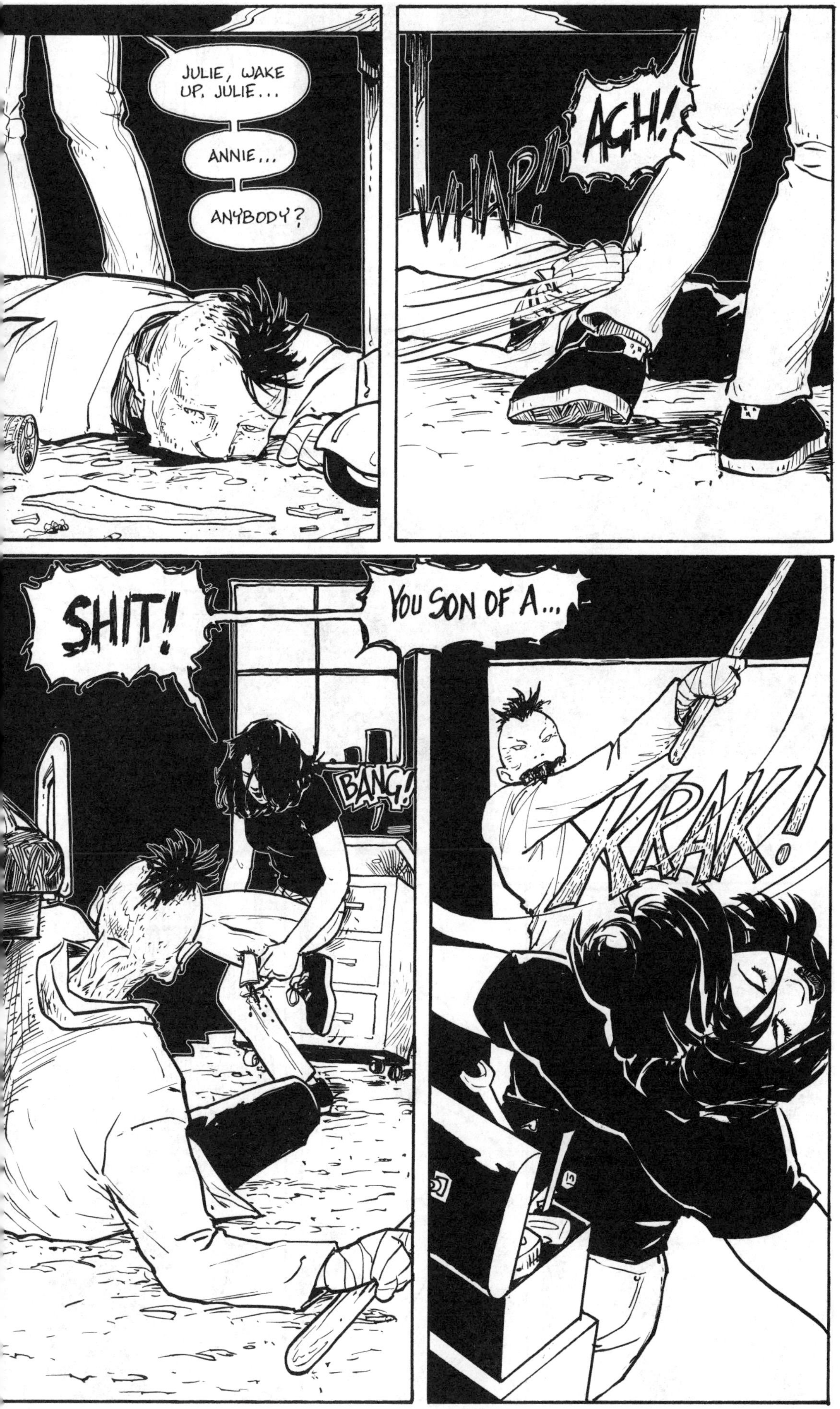

JULIE, WAKE UP, JULIE...
ANNIE...
ANYBODY?
WHAP!!
AGH!
SHIT!
YOU SON OF A...
BANG!
KRAK!

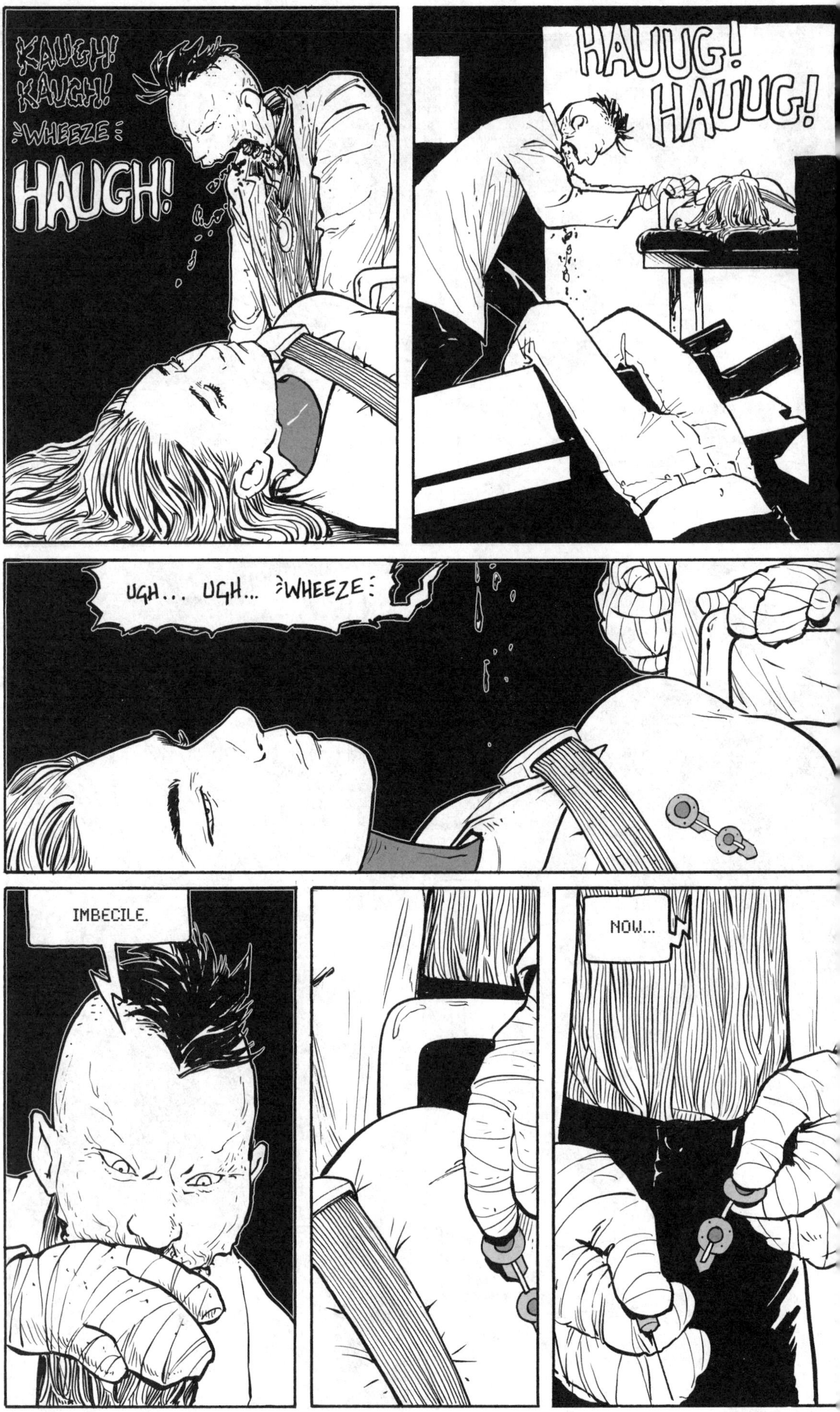
KAUGH! KAUGH!
WHEEZE
HAUGH!
HAUUG! HAUUG!
UGH... UGH... WHEEZE
IMBECILE.
NOW...

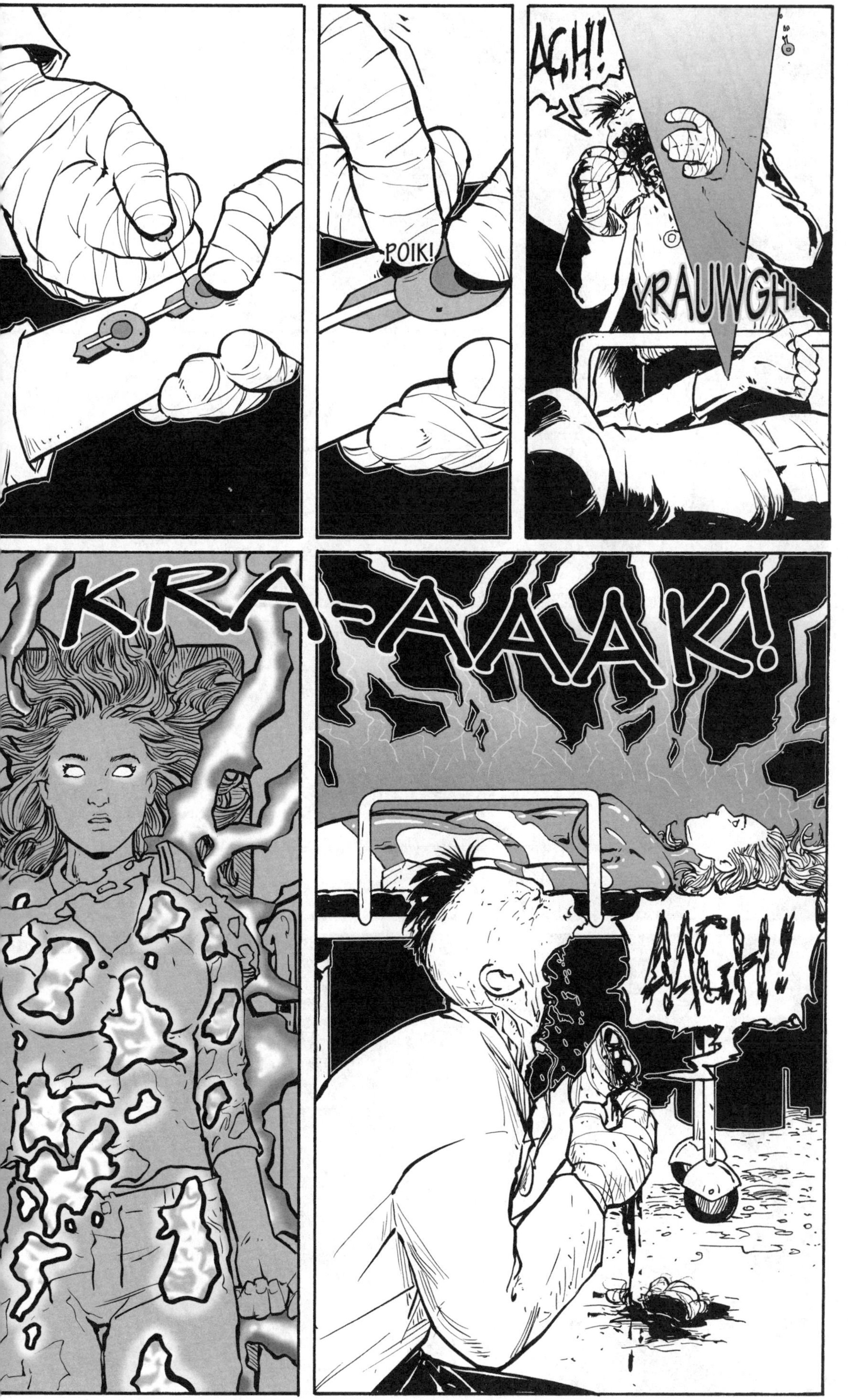
POIK!
AGH!
VRAUWGH!
KRA-AAAK!
AAGH!

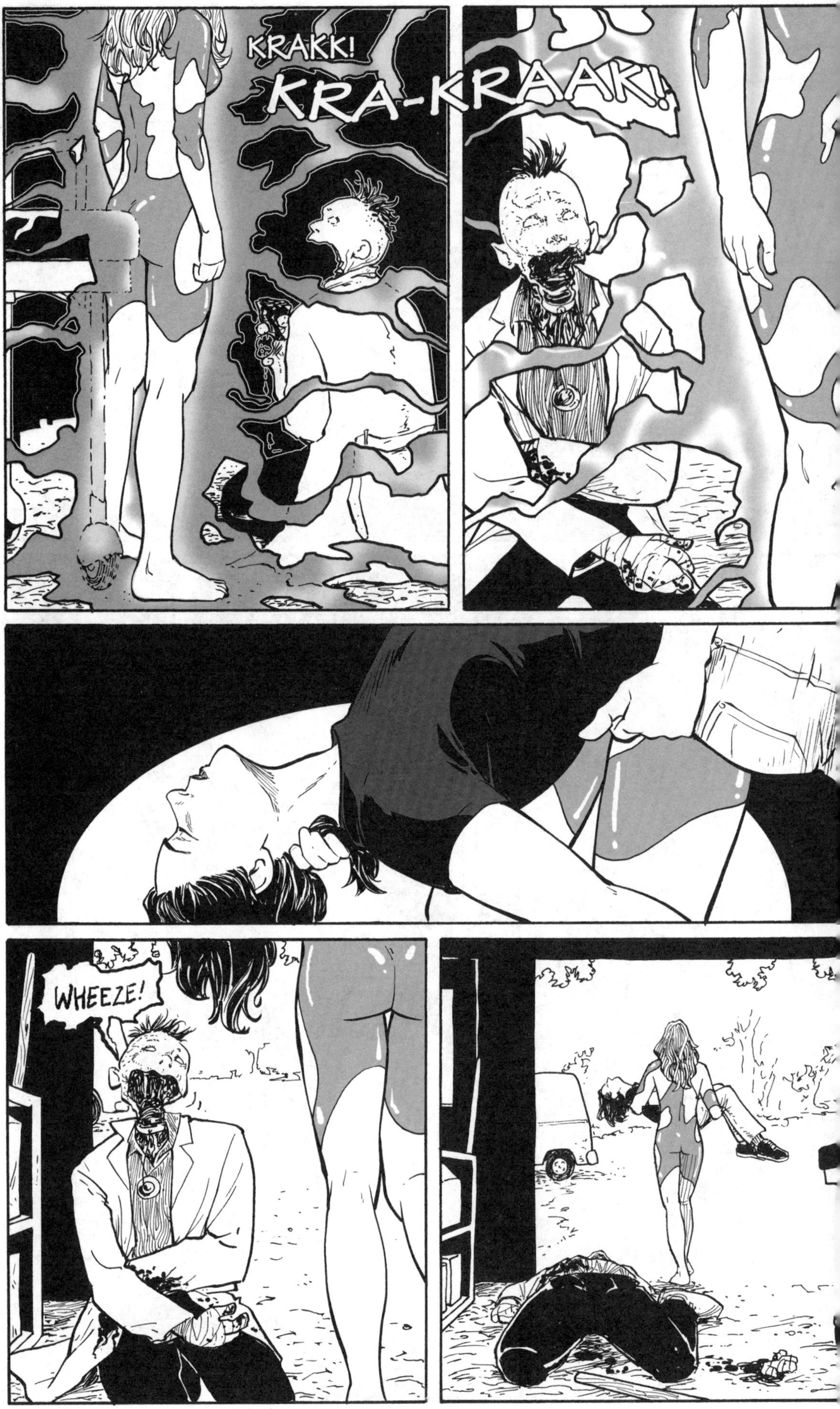
KRAKK!
KRA-KRAAK!
WHEEZE!

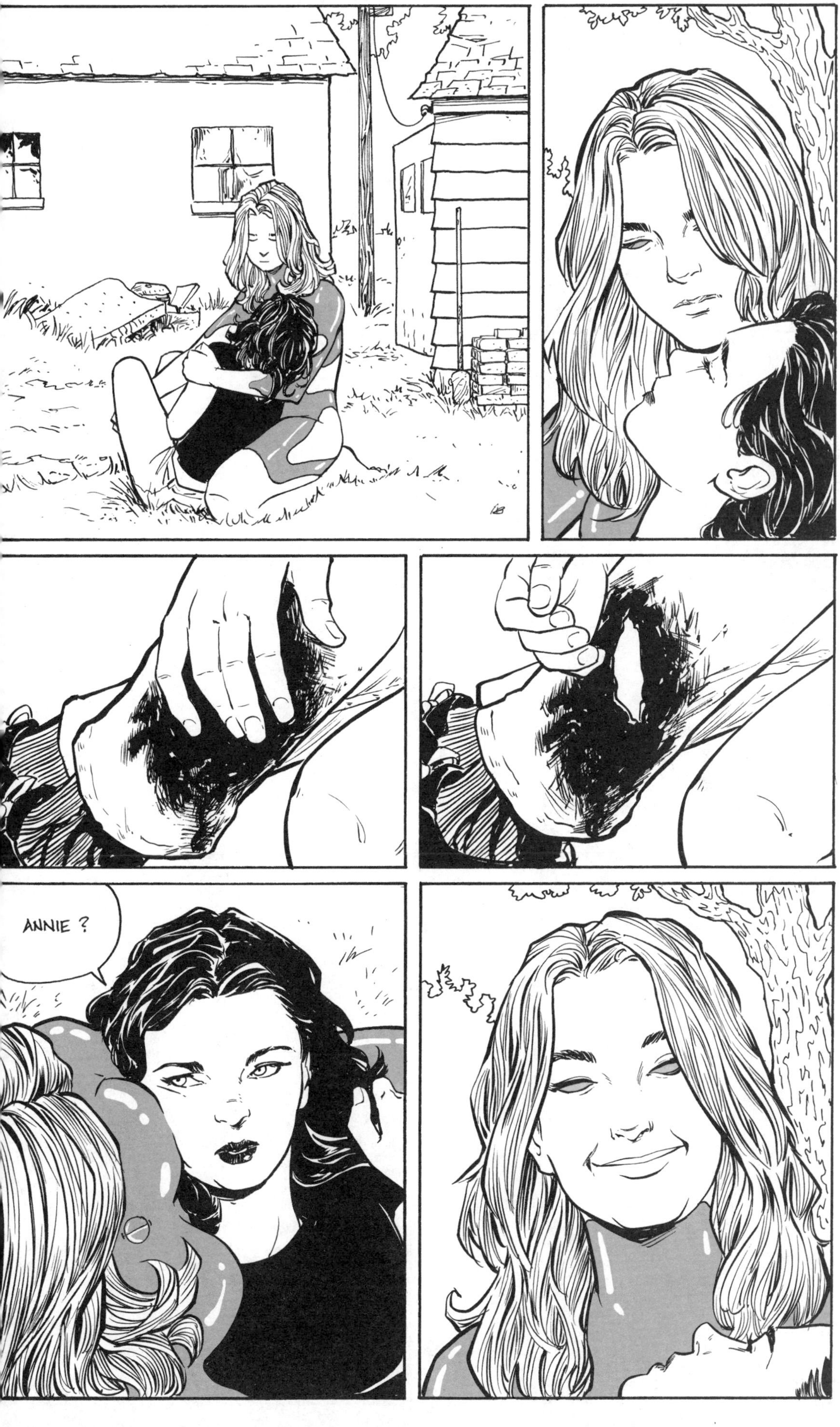
ANNIE ?

"Not only will atomic power be released,
but someday we will harness the rise and fall
of the tides and imprison the rays of the sun"
—Thomas Alva Edison

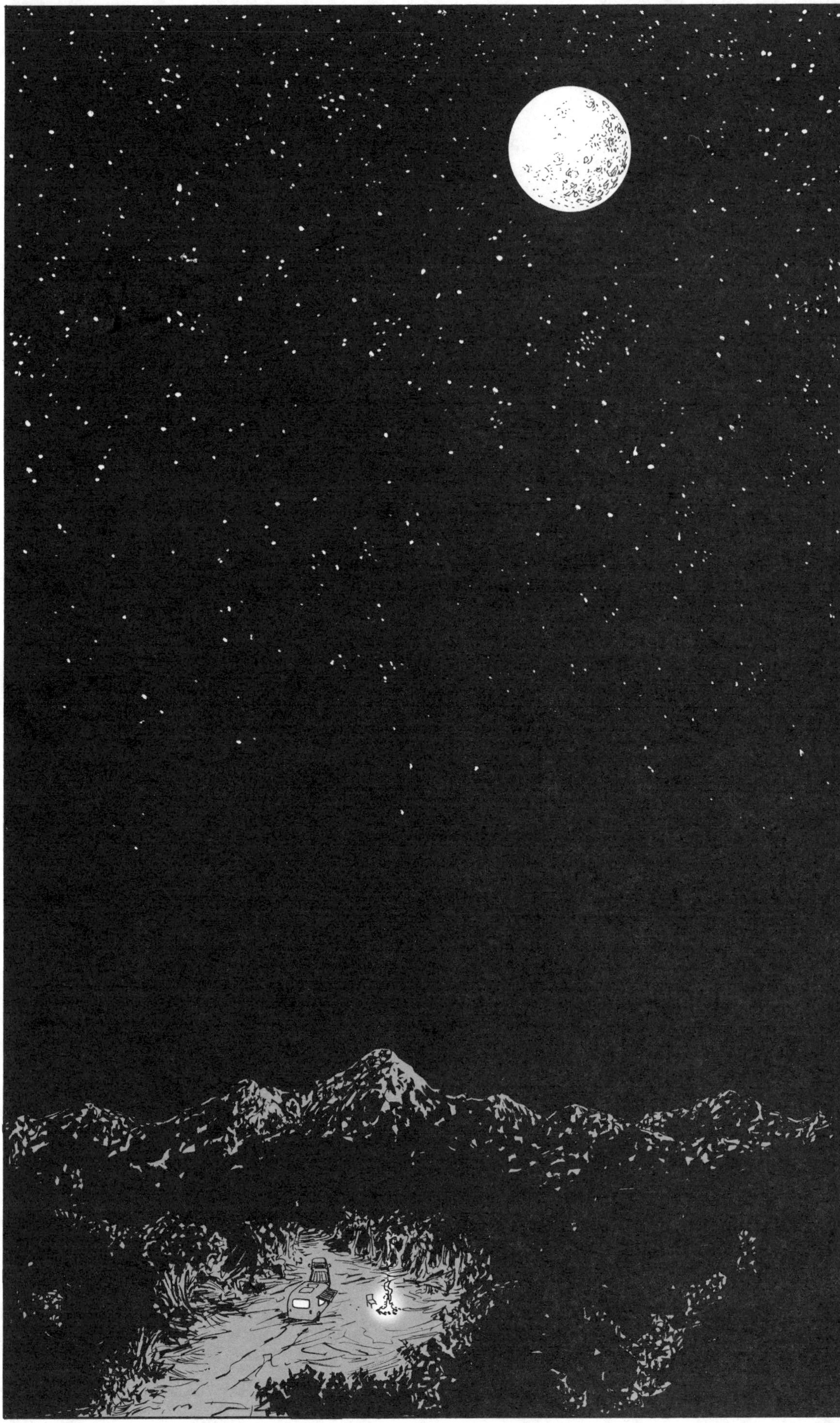

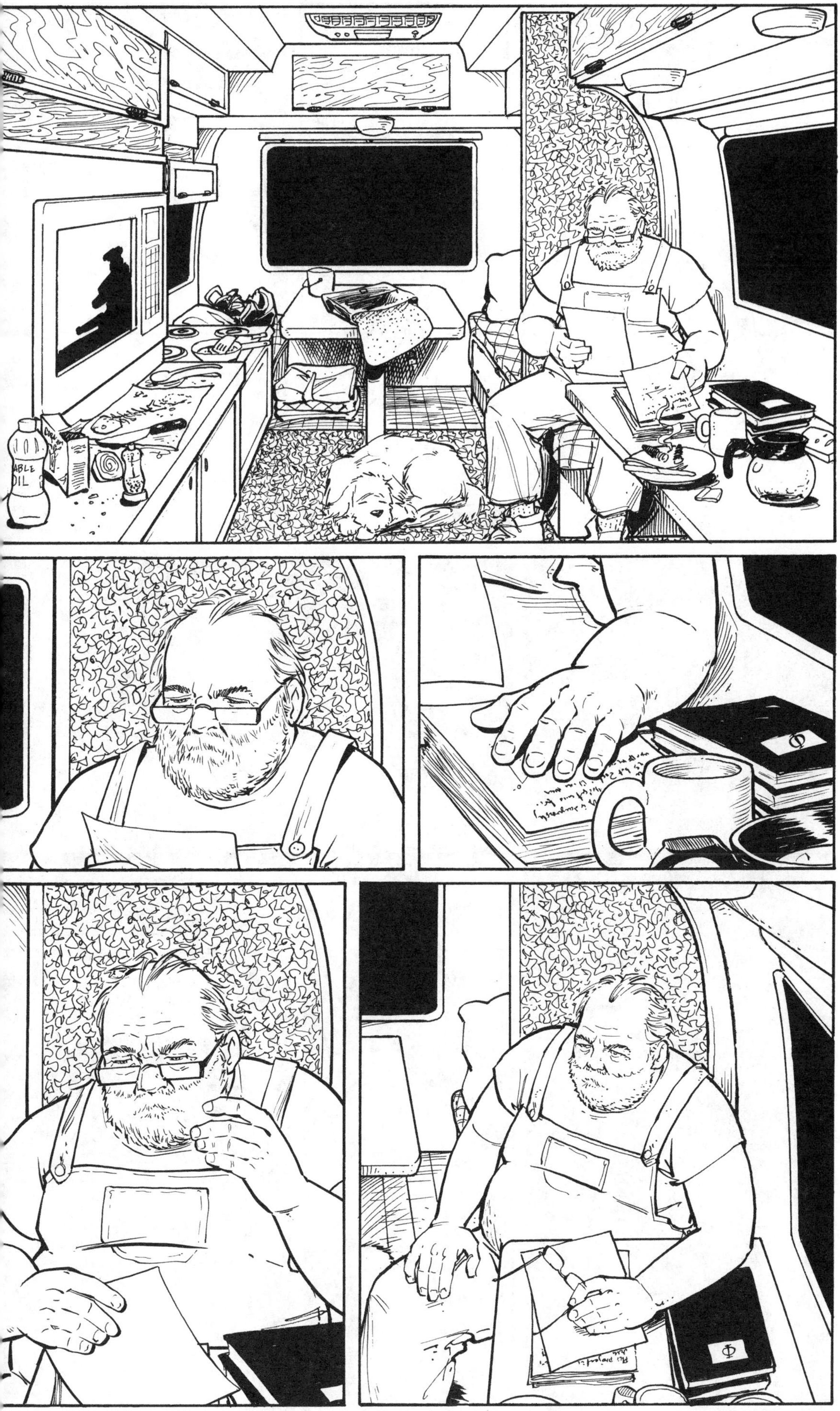

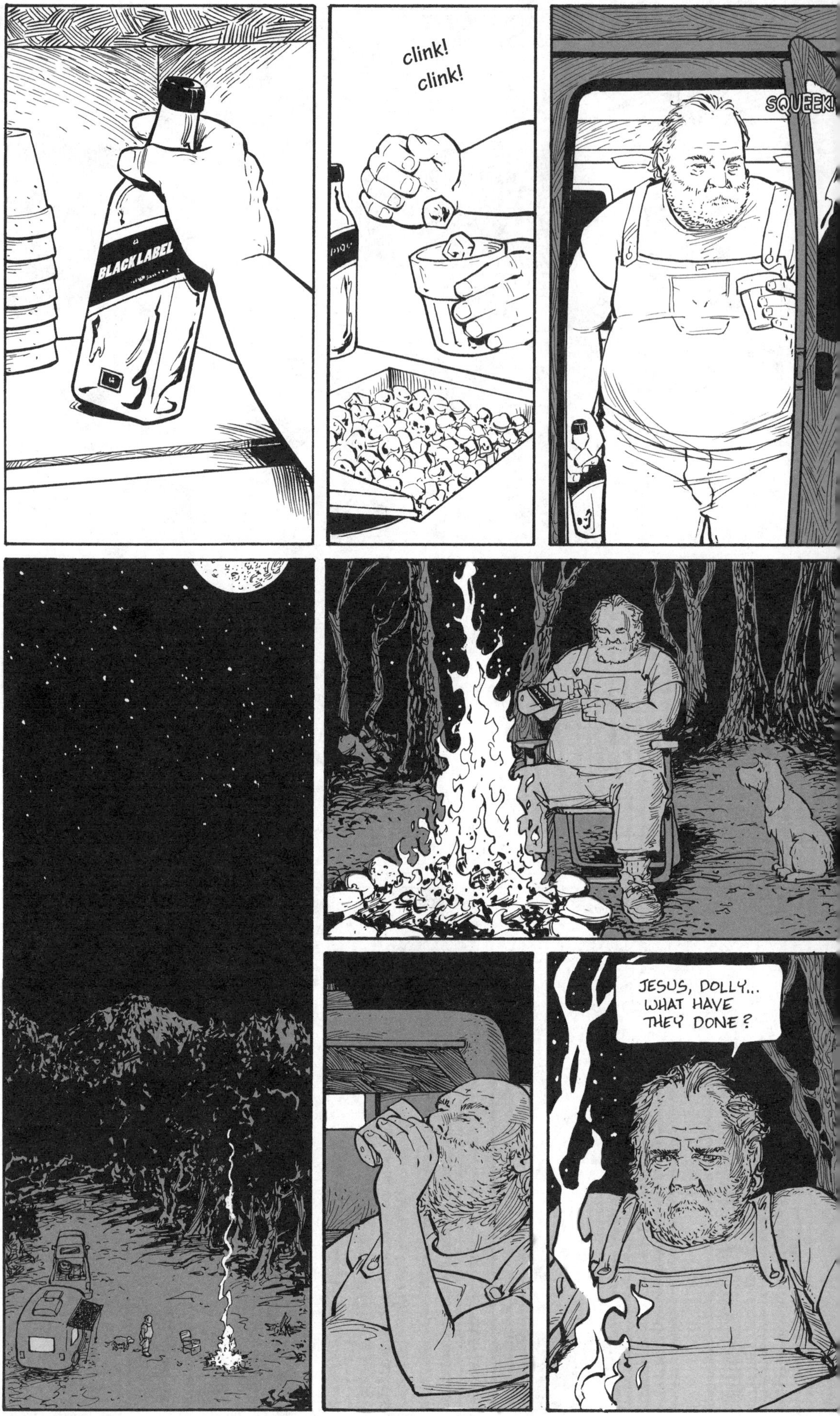
BLACK LABEL
clink!
clink!
SQUEEK!
JESUS, DOLLY...
WHAT HAVE
THEY DONE?

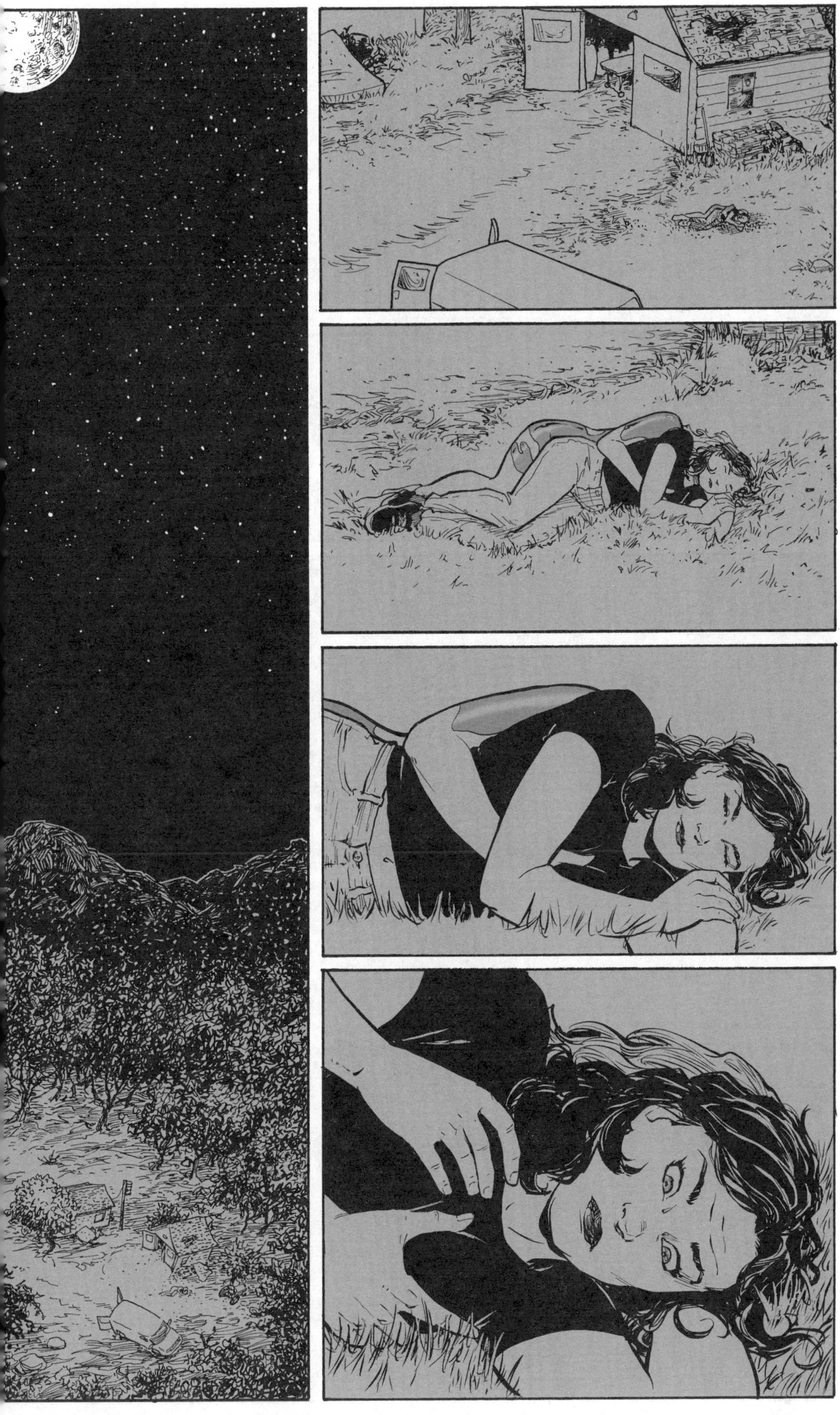

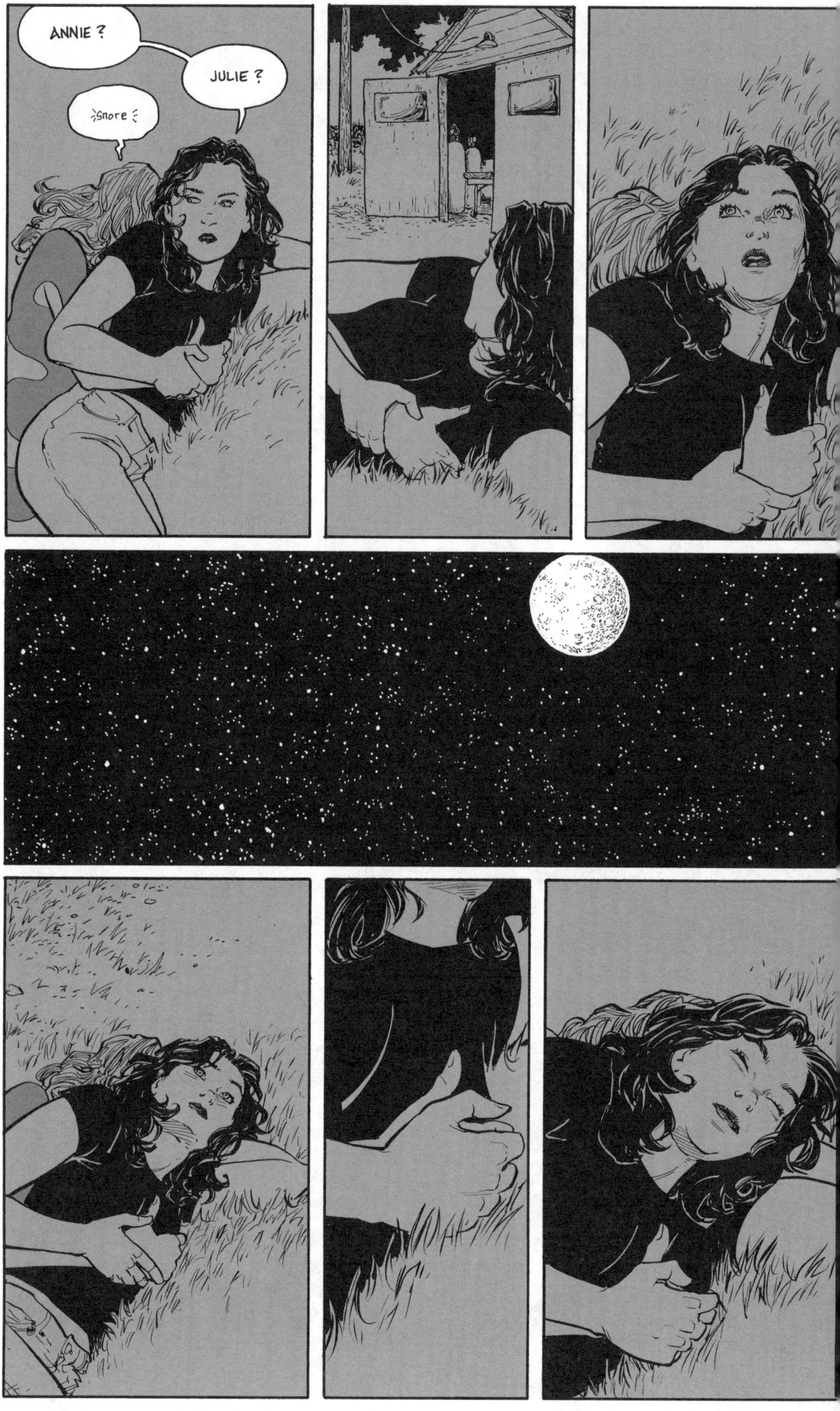
ANNIE ?
JULIE ?
Snore

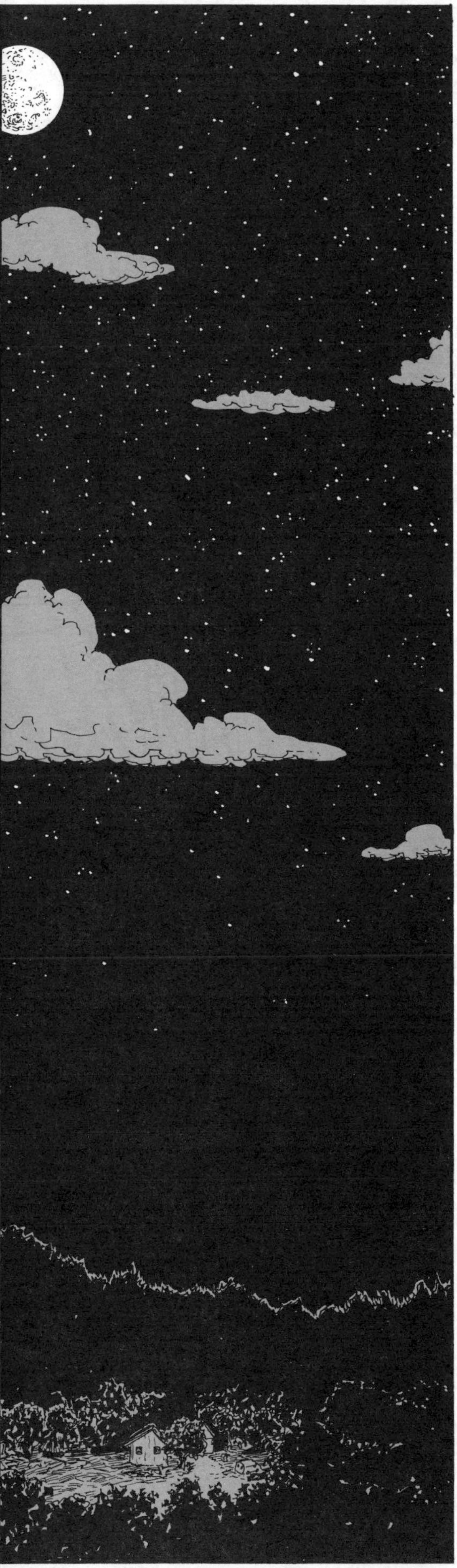
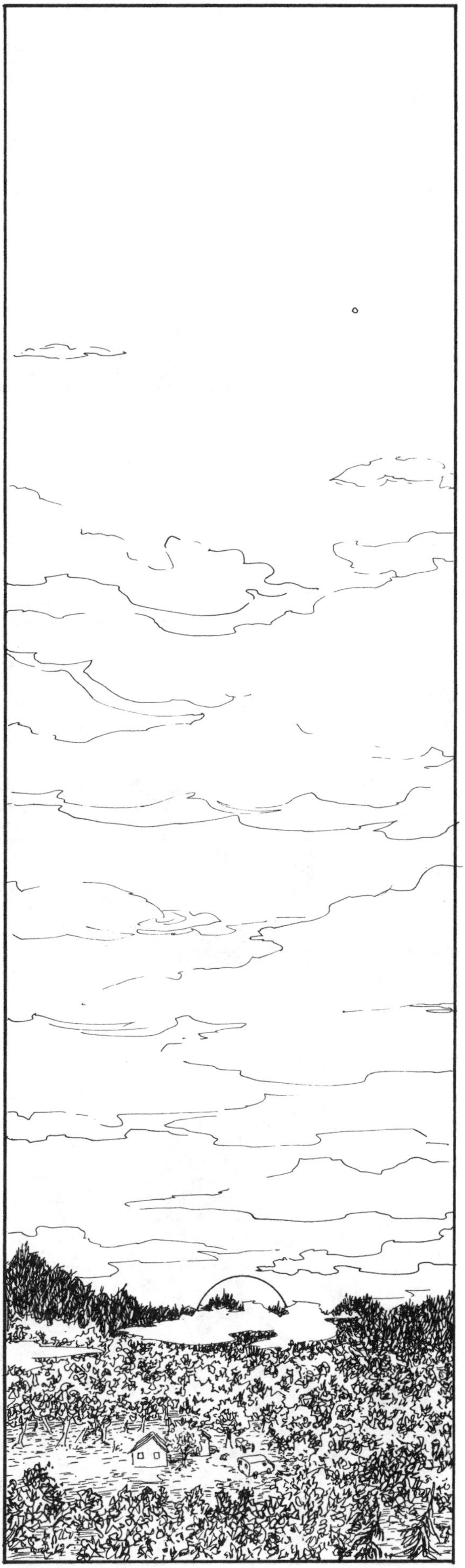

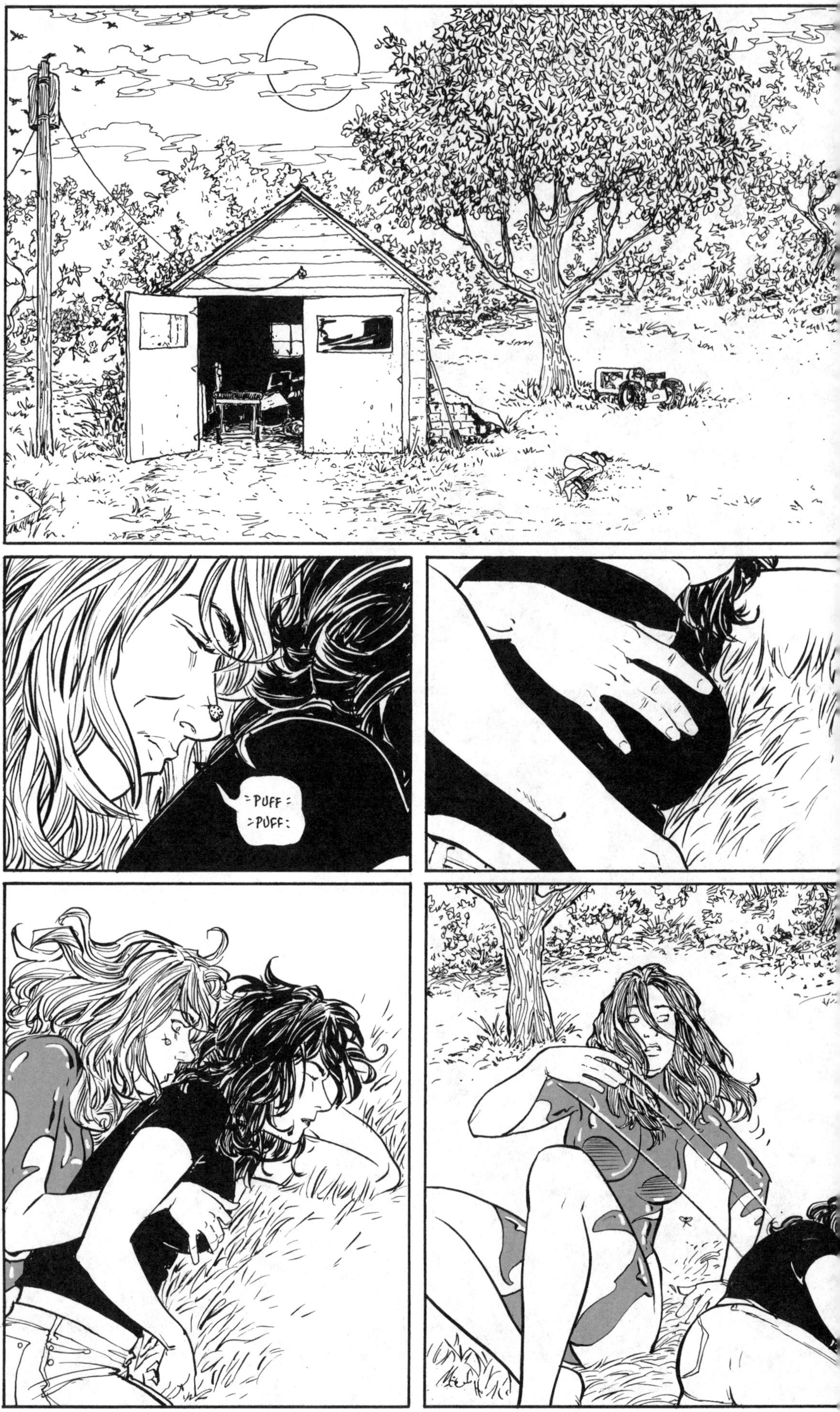
PUFF
PUFF

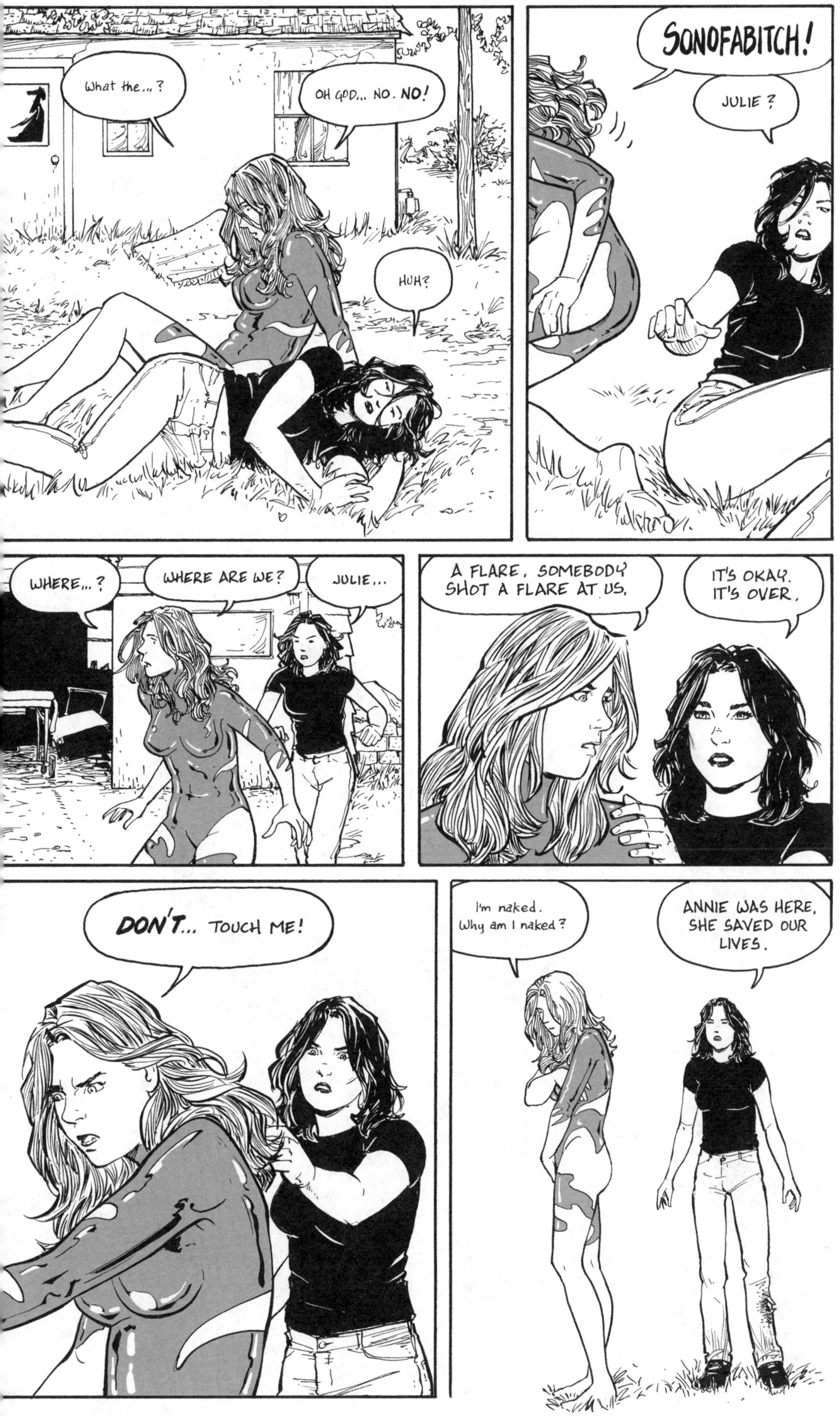
What the...?
OH GOD... NO. NO!
HUH?
SONOFABITCH!
JULIE?
WHERE...?
WHERE ARE WE?
JULIE...
A FLARE. SOMEBODY SHOT A FLARE AT US.
IT'S OKAY. IT'S OVER.
DON'T... TOUCH ME!
I'm naked. Why am I naked?
ANNIE WAS HERE. SHE SAVED OUR LIVES.

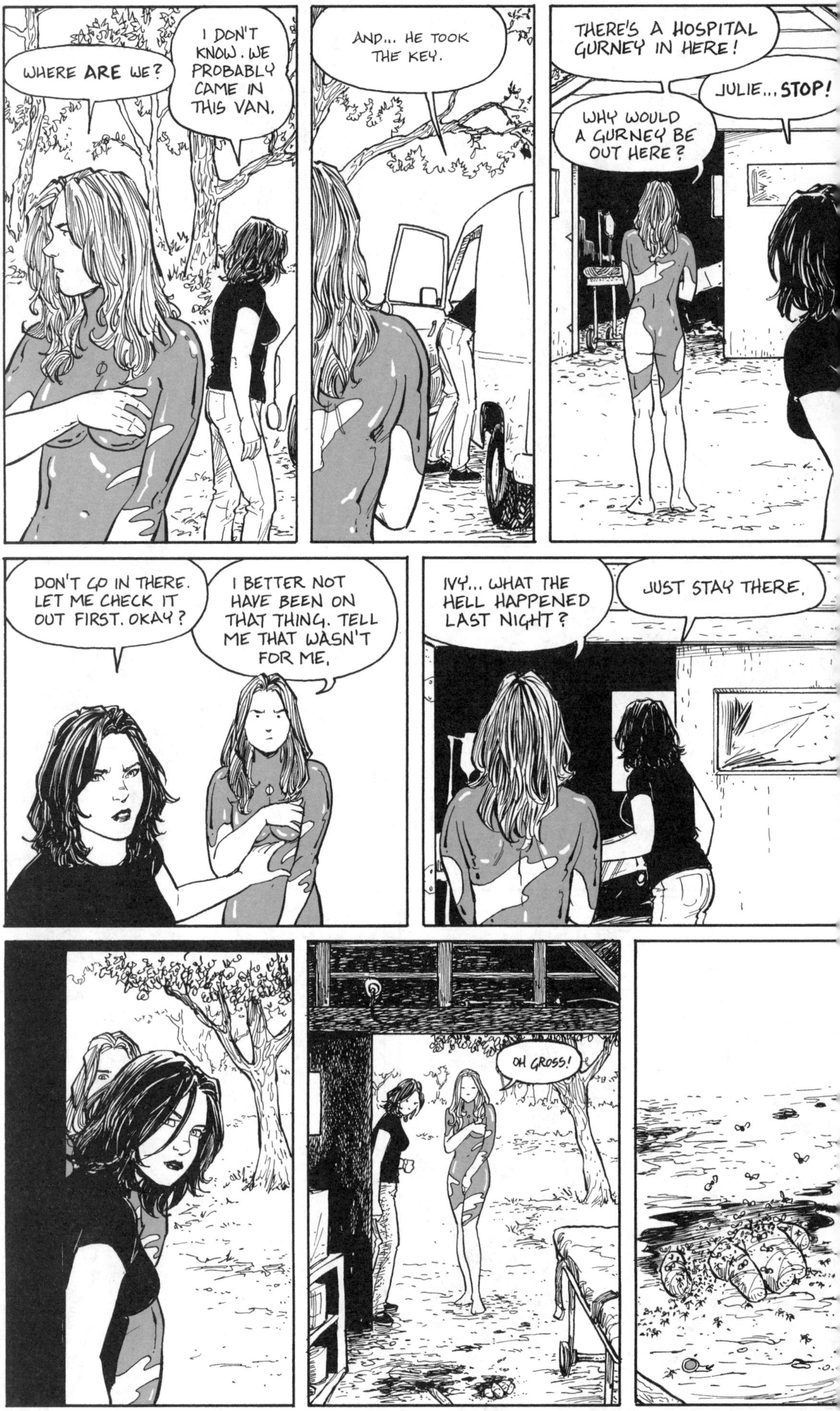
WHERE ARE WE?
I DON'T KNOW. WE PROBABLY CAME IN THIS VAN.
AND... HE TOOK THE KEY.
THERE'S A HOSPITAL GURNEY IN HERE!
WHY WOULD A GURNEY BE OUT HERE?
JULIE... STOP!
DON'T GO IN THERE. LET ME CHECK IT OUT FIRST. OKAY?
I BETTER NOT HAVE BEEN ON THAT THING. TELL ME THAT WASN'T FOR ME.
IVY... WHAT THE HELL HAPPENED LAST NIGHT?
JUST STAY THERE.
OH GROSS!

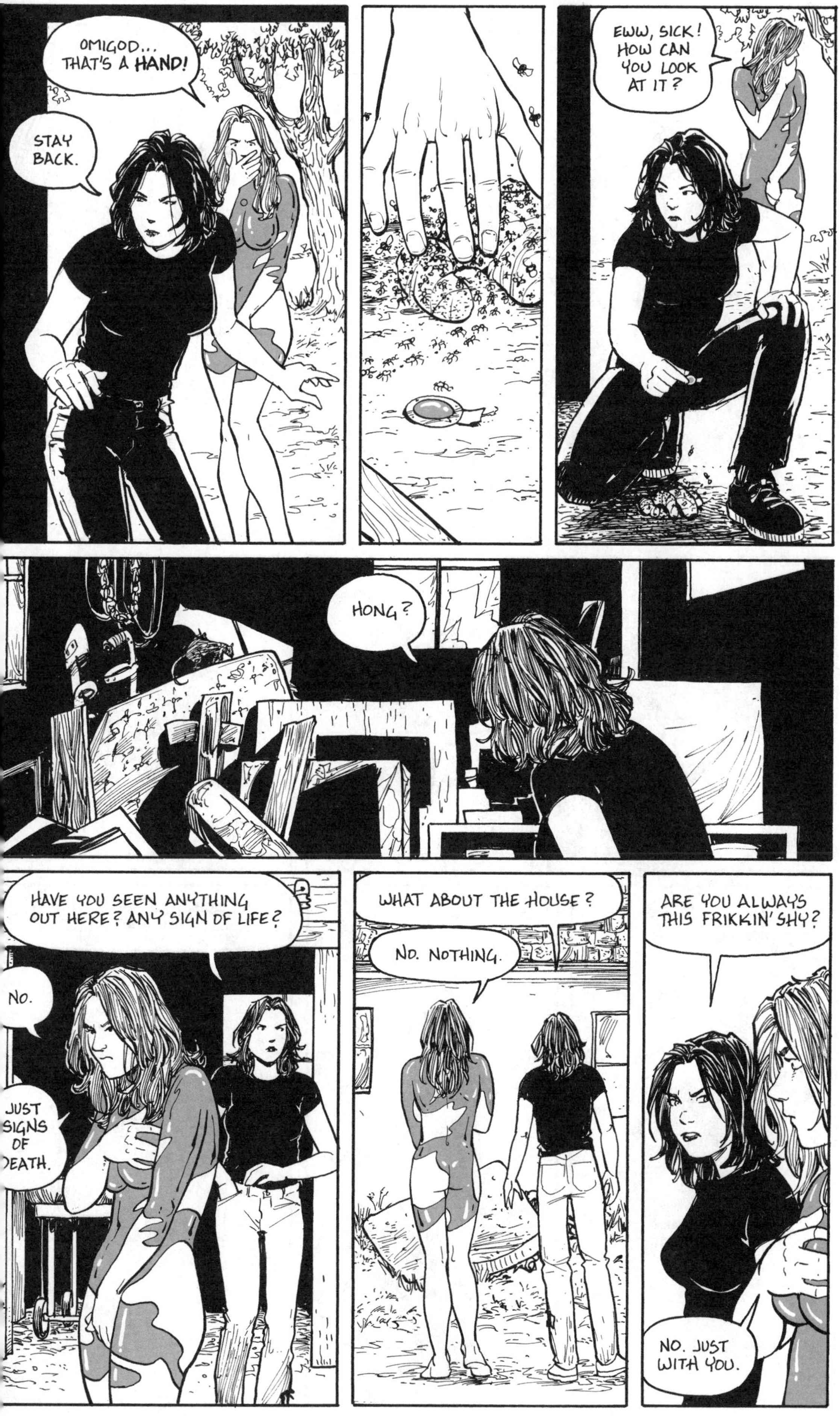
OMIGOD... THAT'S A HAND!
STAY BACK.
EWW, SICK! HOW CAN YOU LOOK AT IT?
HONG?
HAVE YOU SEEN ANYTHING OUT HERE? ANY SIGN OF LIFE?
NO.
JUST SIGNS OF DEATH.
WHAT ABOUT THE HOUSE?
NO. NOTHING.
ARE YOU ALWAYS THIS FRIKKIN' SHY?
NO. JUST WITH YOU.

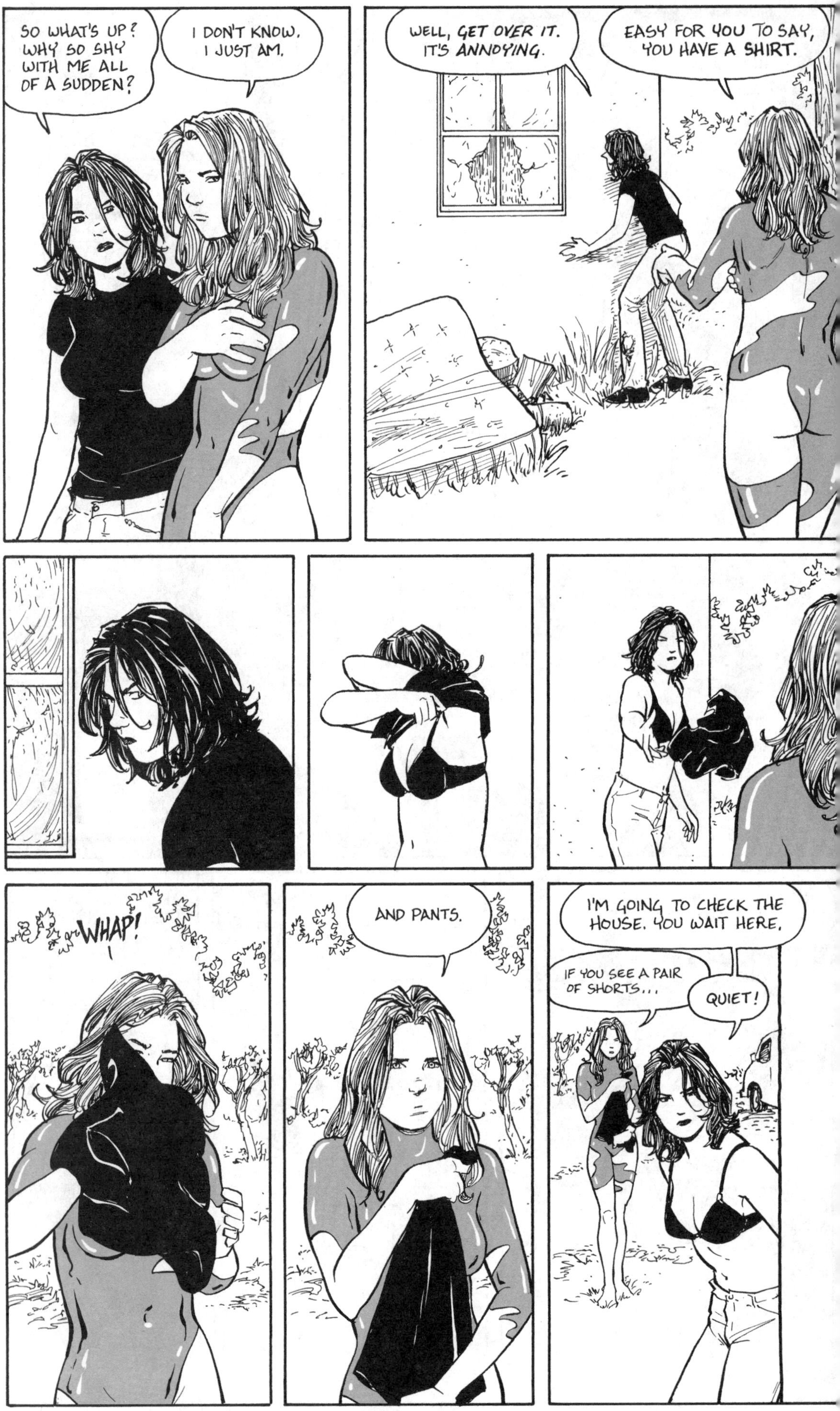
SO WHAT'S UP? WHY SO SHY WITH ME ALL OF A SUDDEN?
I DON'T KNOW. I JUST AM.
WELL, GET OVER IT. IT'S ANNOYING.
EASY FOR YOU TO SAY, YOU HAVE A SHIRT.
WHAP!
AND PANTS.
I'M GOING TO CHECK THE HOUSE. YOU WAIT HERE.
IF YOU SEE A PAIR OF SHORTS...
QUIET!

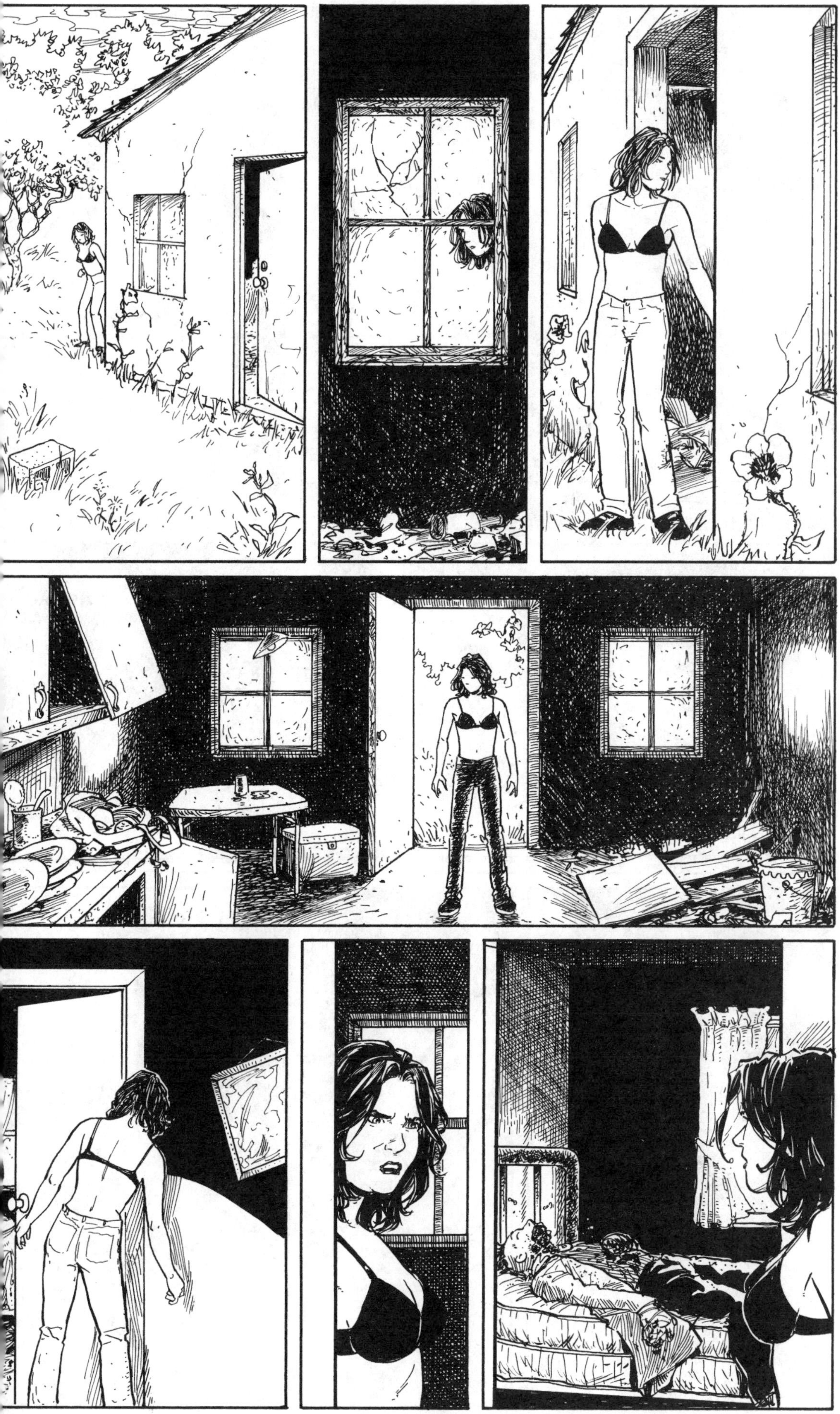

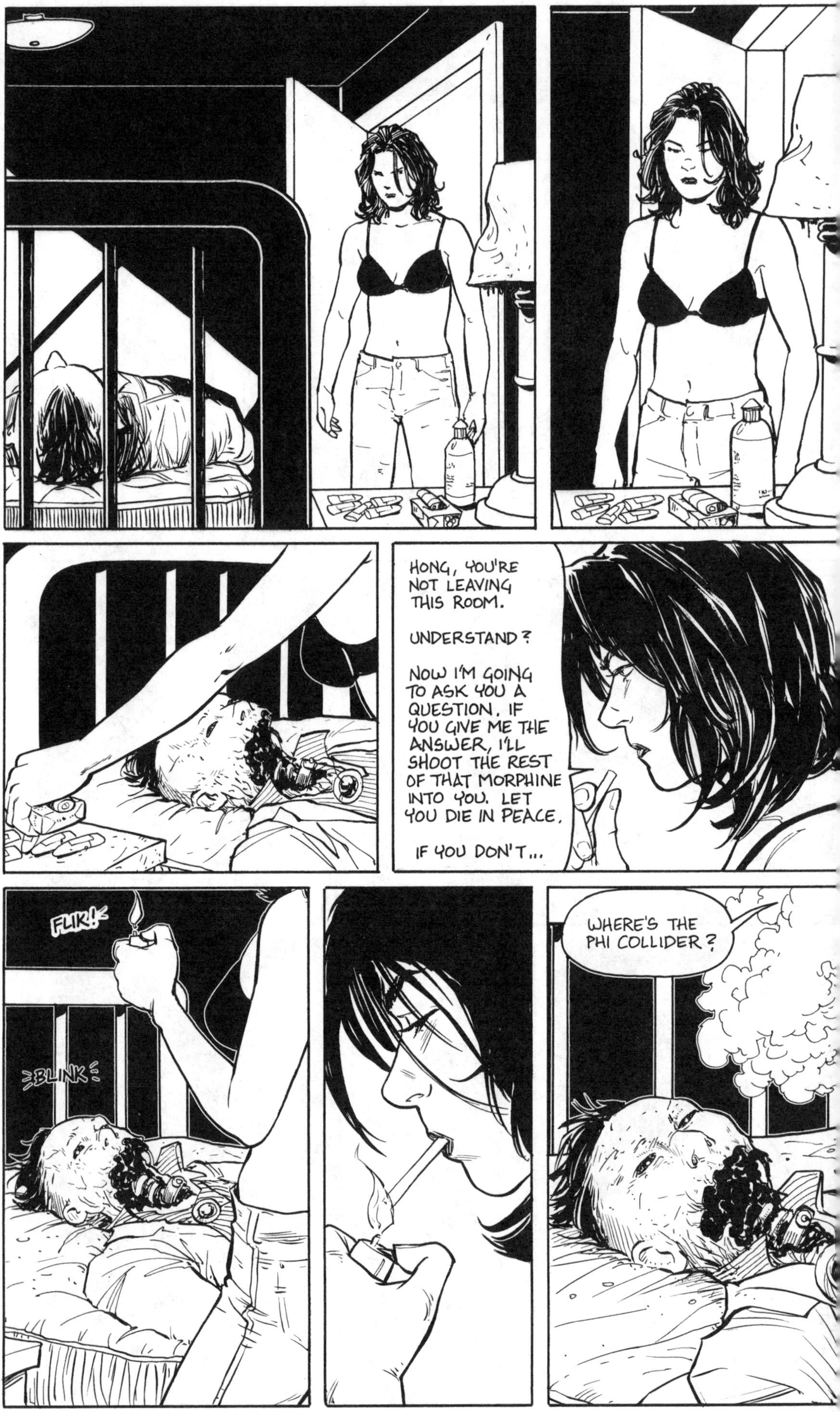
HONG, YOU'RE NOT LEAVING THIS ROOM.
UNDERSTAND?
NOW I'M GOING TO ASK YOU A QUESTION. IF YOU GIVE ME THE ANSWER, I'LL SHOOT THE REST OF THAT MORPHINE INTO YOU. LET YOU DIE IN PEACE.
IF YOU DON'T...
FLIK!
BLINK
WHERE'S THE PHI COLLIDER?

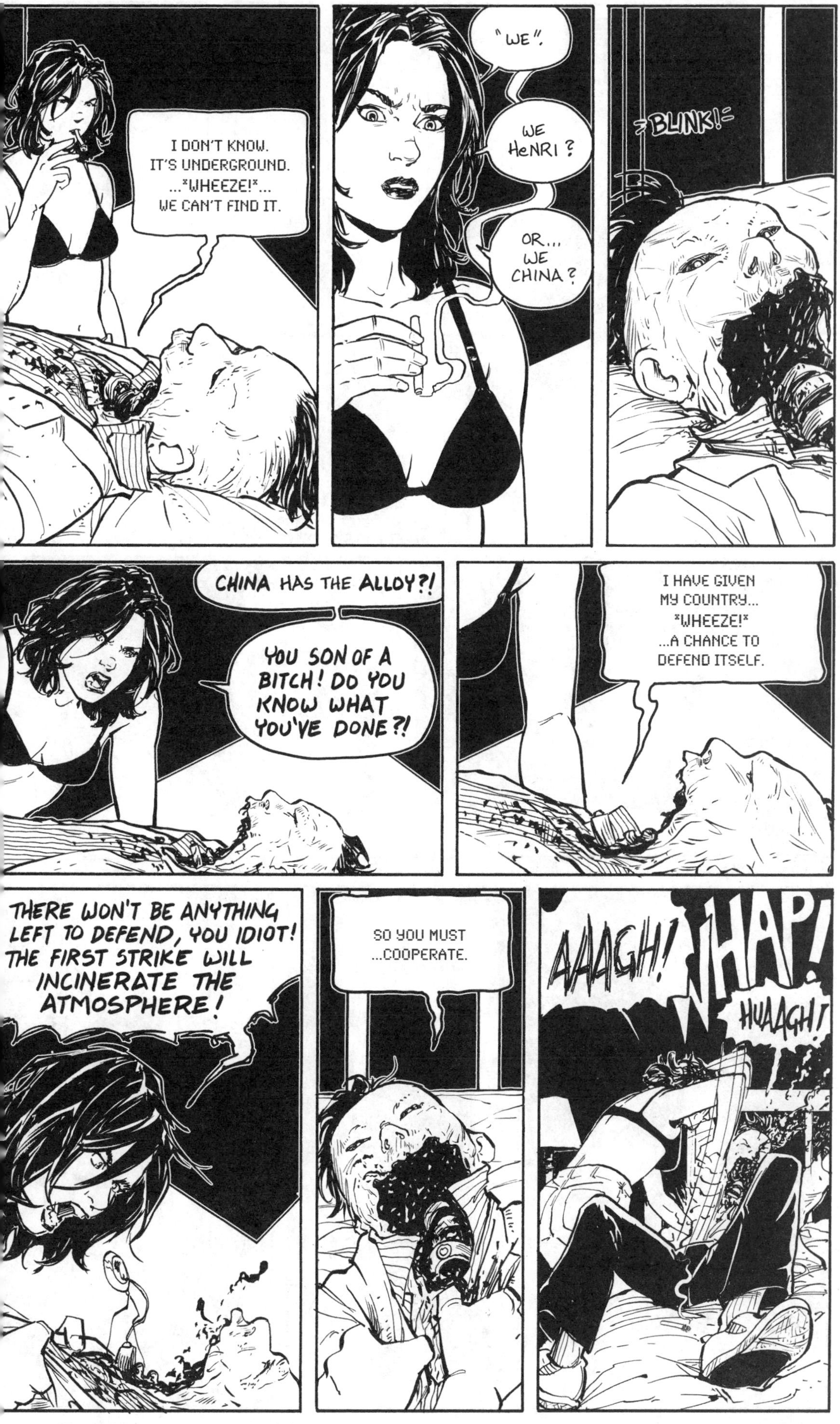
I DON'T KNOW. IT'S UNDERGROUND. ...*WHEEZE!*... WE CAN'T FIND IT.
"WE".
WE HeNRI ?
OR... WE CHINA ?
BLINK!
CHINA HAS THE ALLOY?!
YOU SON OF A BITCH! DO YOU KNOW WHAT YOU'VE DONE?!
I HAVE GIVEN MY COUNTRY... *WHEEZE!* ...A CHANCE TO DEFEND ITSELF.
THERE WON'T BE ANYTHING LEFT TO DEFEND, YOU IDIOT! THE FIRST STRIKE WILL INCINERATE THE ATMOSPHERE!
SO YOU MUST ...COOPERATE.
AAAGH!
JHAP!
HUAAGH!

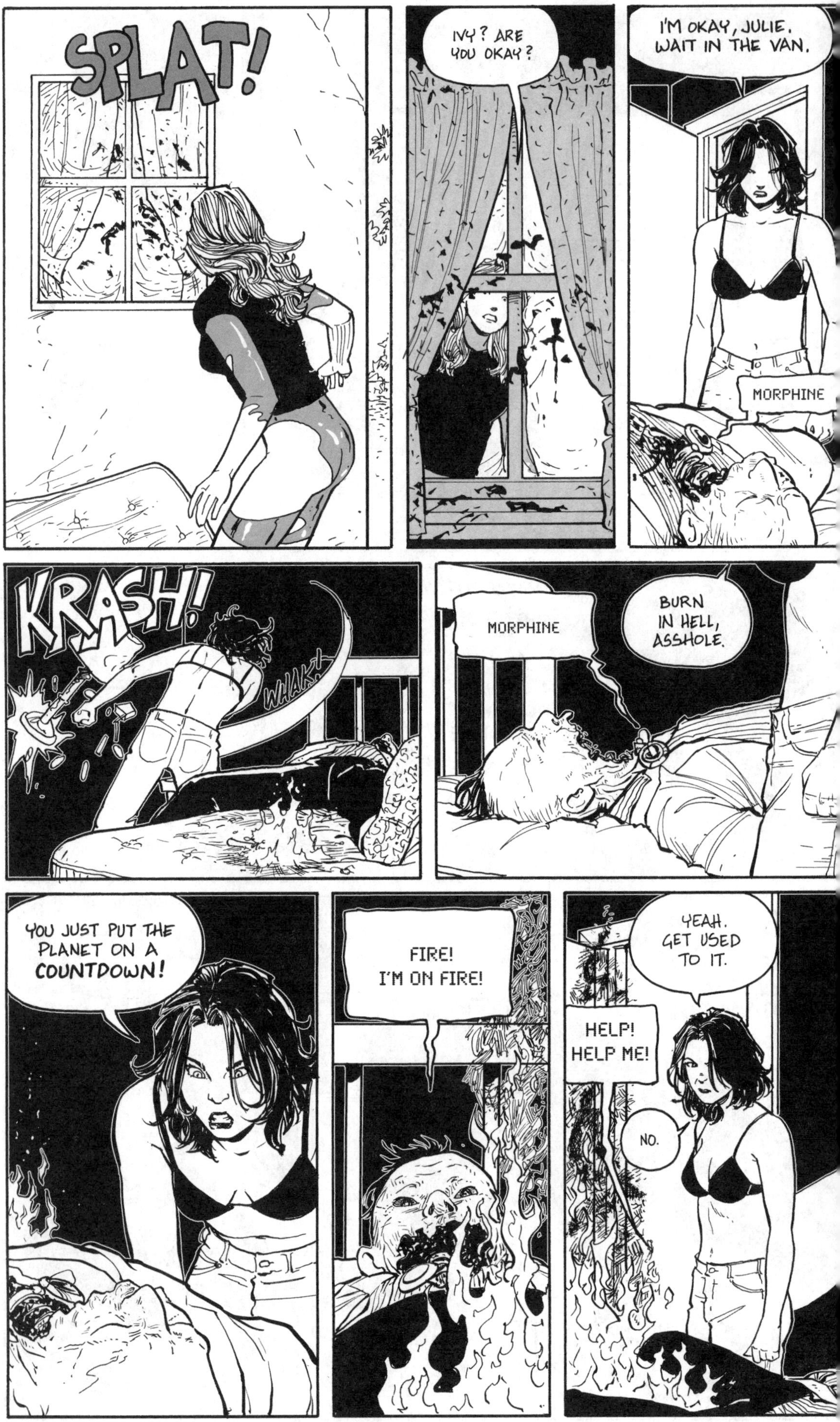
SPLAT!
IVY? ARE YOU OKAY?
I'M OKAY, JULIE. WAIT IN THE VAN.
MORPHINE
KRASH!
WHAK!
MORPHINE
BURN IN HELL, ASSHOLE.
YOU JUST PUT THE PLANET ON A COUNTDOWN!
FIRE! I'M ON FIRE!
YEAH. GET USED TO IT.
HELP! HELP ME!
NO.

AAAEIGH!!

OH, CRAP!

SNAP!

COME BACK! I'LL TALK!

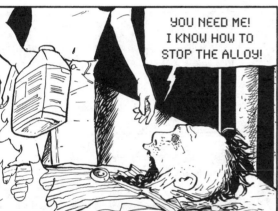

YOU NEED ME! I KNOW HOW TO STOP THE ALLOY!

NOOO!

MINERAL SPIRITS

SAVE ME! I'M BURNING! WHAT ARE YOU DOING?

FORGOT MY KEYS.

NO!

WITHOUT ME YOU'RE ALL GOING TO DIE! EVERYBODY WILL DIIIEEE!!!

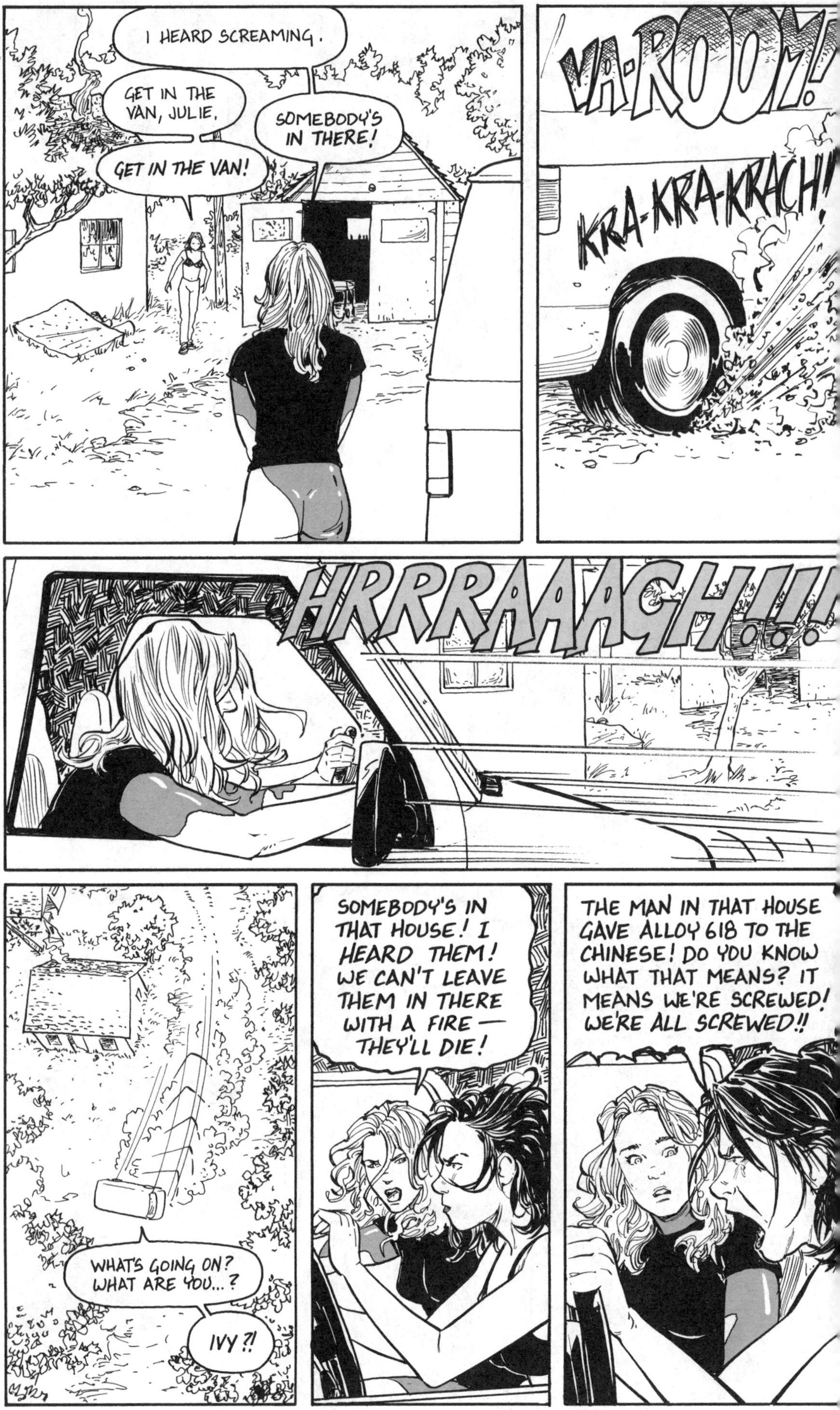
I HEARD SCREAMING.
GET IN THE VAN, JULIE.
SOMEBODY'S IN THERE!
GET IN THE VAN!
VA-ROOOM!
KRA-KRA-KRACH!!
HRRRAAAGH!!!
WHAT'S GOING ON? WHAT ARE YOU...?
IVY?!
SOMEBODY'S IN THAT HOUSE! I HEARD THEM! WE CAN'T LEAVE THEM IN THERE WITH A FIRE— THEY'LL DIE!
THE MAN IN THAT HOUSE GAVE ALLOY 618 TO THE CHINESE! DO YOU KNOW WHAT THAT MEANS? IT MEANS WE'RE SCREWED! WE'RE ALL SCREWED!!

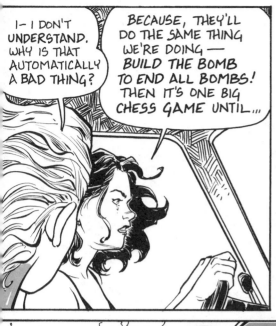

I— I DON'T UNDERSTAND. WHY IS THAT AUTOMATICALLY A BAD THING?

BECAUSE, THEY'LL DO THE SAME THING WE'RE DOING — BUILD THE BOMB TO END ALL BOMBS! THEN IT'S ONE BIG CHESS GAME UNTIL....

WE'RE BUILDING A BOMB WITH ANNIE'S ALLOY?

OF COURSE WE ARE! WHAT'S THE FIRST THING WE DID WITH ATOMIC ENERGY? THE VERY FIRST THING?

BOOM!

CHECKMATE.

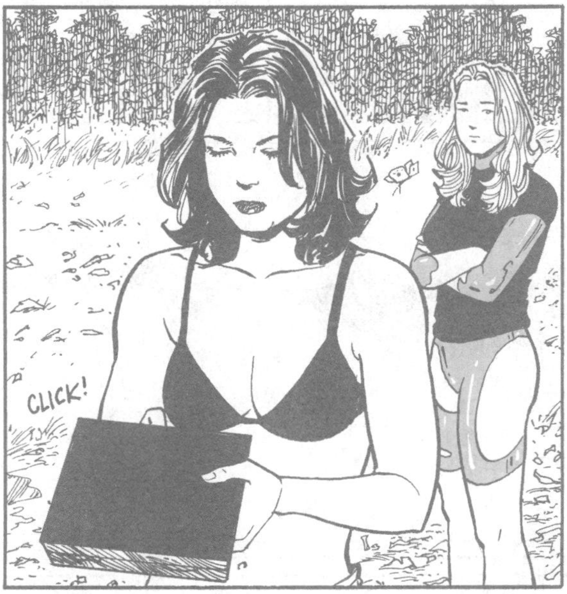
CLICK!

"Igitur qui desiderat pacem, praeparet bellum."
—Vegetius

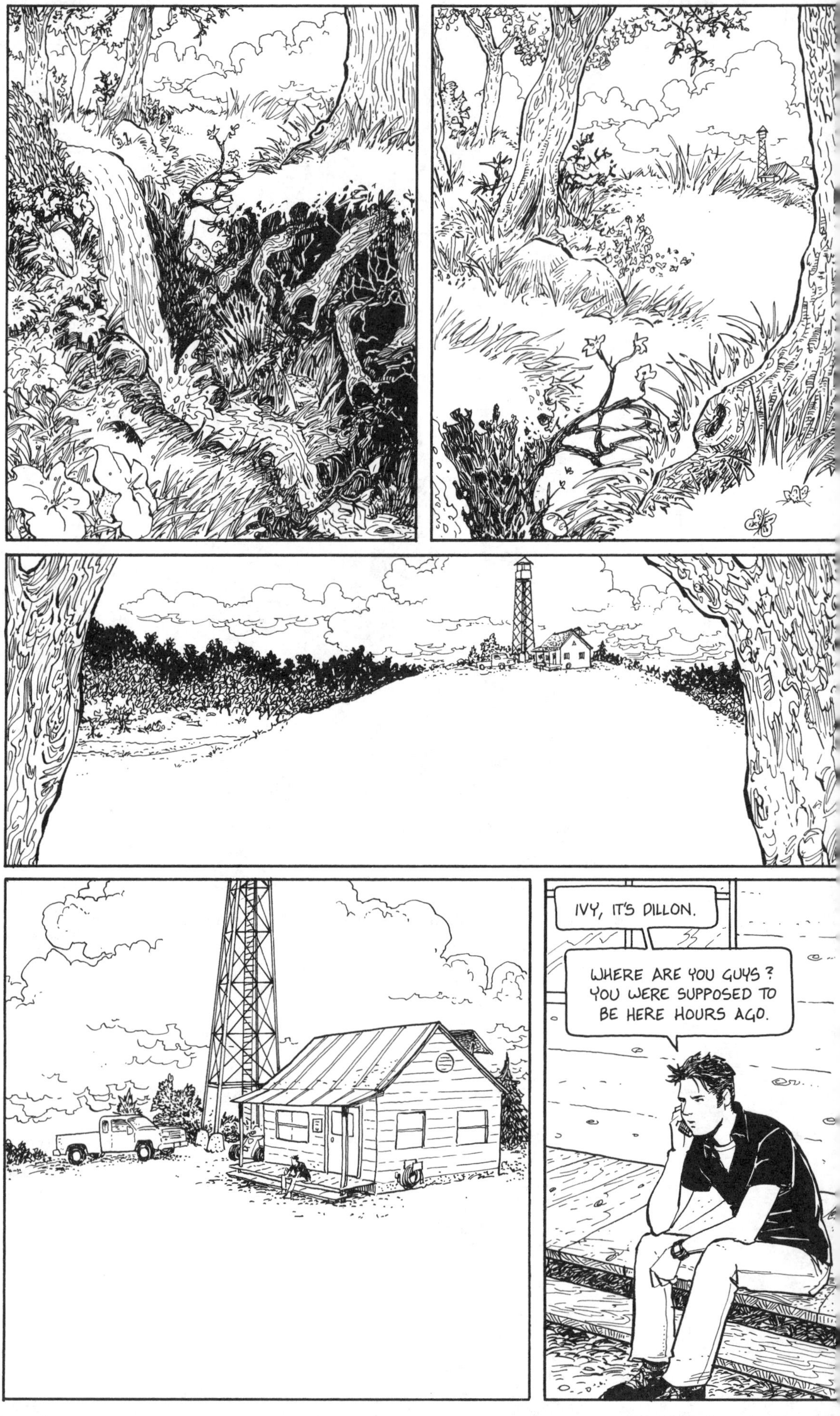
IVY, IT'S DILLON.
WHERE ARE YOU GUYS? YOU WERE SUPPOSED TO BE HERE HOURS AGO.

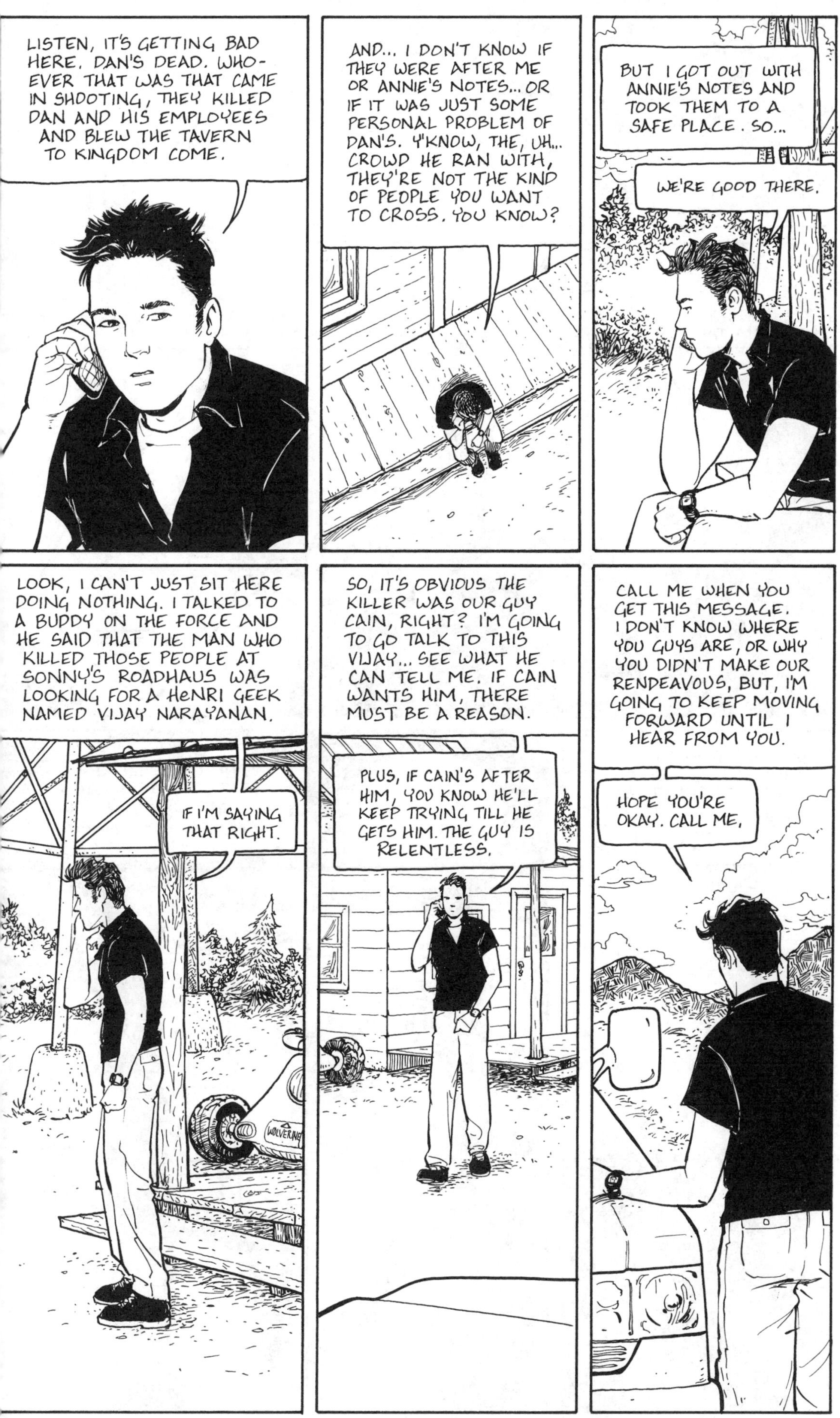
LISTEN, IT'S GETTING BAD HERE. DAN'S DEAD. WHOEVER THAT WAS THAT CAME IN SHOOTING, THEY KILLED DAN AND HIS EMPLOYEES AND BLEW THE TAVERN TO KINGDOM COME.
AND... I DON'T KNOW IF THEY WERE AFTER ME OR ANNIE'S NOTES... OR IF IT WAS JUST SOME PERSONAL PROBLEM OF DAN'S. Y'KNOW, THE, UH... CROWD HE RAN WITH, THEY'RE NOT THE KIND OF PEOPLE YOU WANT TO CROSS. YOU KNOW?
BUT I GOT OUT WITH ANNIE'S NOTES AND TOOK THEM TO A SAFE PLACE. SO...
WE'RE GOOD THERE.
LOOK, I CAN'T JUST SIT HERE DOING NOTHING. I TALKED TO A BUDDY ON THE FORCE AND HE SAID THAT THE MAN WHO KILLED THOSE PEOPLE AT SONNY'S ROADHAUS WAS LOOKING FOR A HeNRI GEEK NAMED VIJAY NARAYANAN.
IF I'M SAYING THAT RIGHT.
SO, IT'S OBVIOUS THE KILLER WAS OUR GUY CAIN, RIGHT? I'M GOING TO GO TALK TO THIS VIJAY... SEE WHAT HE CAN TELL ME. IF CAIN WANTS HIM, THERE MUST BE A REASON.
PLUS, IF CAIN'S AFTER HIM, YOU KNOW HE'LL KEEP TRYING TILL HE GETS HIM. THE GUY IS RELENTLESS.
CALL ME WHEN YOU GET THIS MESSAGE. I DON'T KNOW WHERE YOU GUYS ARE, OR WHY YOU DIDN'T MAKE OUR RENDEAVOUS, BUT, I'M GOING TO KEEP MOVING FORWARD UNTIL I HEAR FROM YOU.
HOPE YOU'RE OKAY. CALL ME.
WOLVERINE

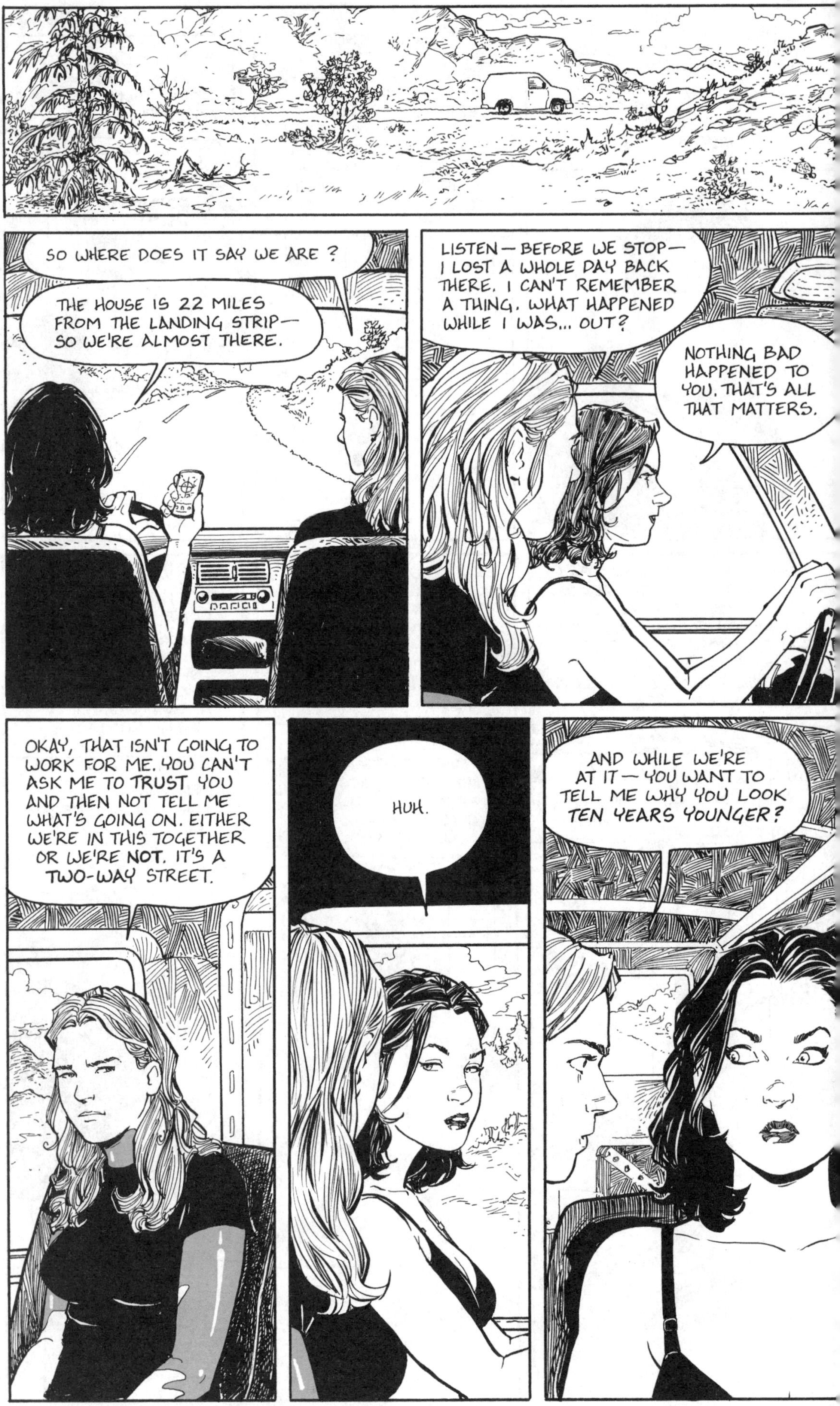
SO WHERE DOES IT SAY WE ARE ?
THE HOUSE IS 22 MILES FROM THE LANDING STRIP— SO WE'RE ALMOST THERE.
LISTEN—BEFORE WE STOP— I LOST A WHOLE DAY BACK THERE. I CAN'T REMEMBER A THING. WHAT HAPPENED WHILE I WAS... OUT?
NOTHING BAD HAPPENED TO YOU. THAT'S ALL THAT MATTERS.
OKAY, THAT ISN'T GOING TO WORK FOR ME. YOU CAN'T ASK ME TO TRUST YOU AND THEN NOT TELL ME WHAT'S GOING ON. EITHER WE'RE IN THIS TOGETHER OR WE'RE NOT. IT'S A TWO-WAY STREET.
HUH.
AND WHILE WE'RE AT IT—YOU WANT TO TELL ME WHY YOU LOOK TEN YEARS YOUNGER?

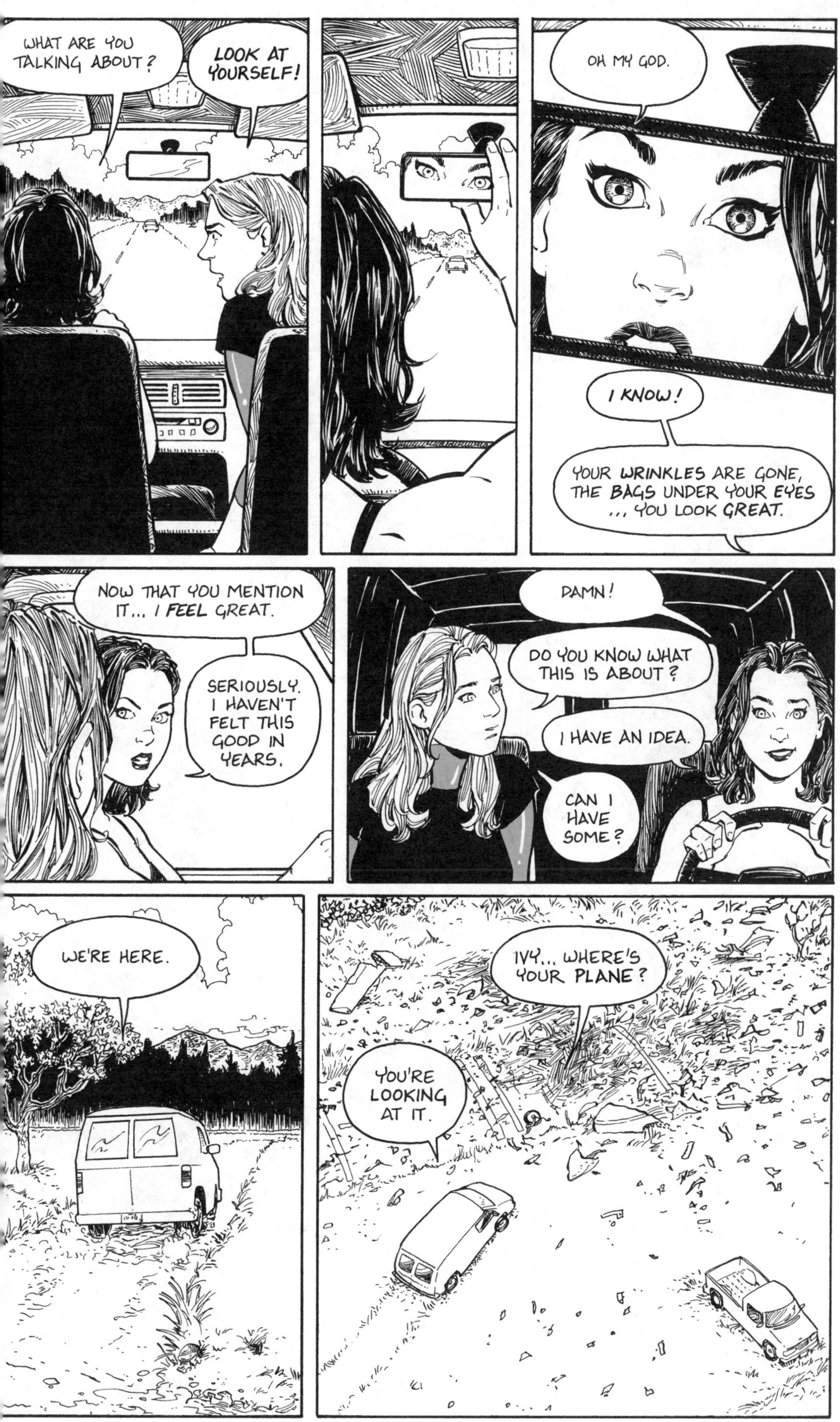
WHAT ARE YOU TALKING ABOUT?
LOOK AT YOURSELF!
OH MY GOD.
I KNOW!
YOUR WRINKLES ARE GONE, THE BAGS UNDER YOUR EYES ... YOU LOOK GREAT.
NOW THAT YOU MENTION IT... I FEEL GREAT.
SERIOUSLY. I HAVEN'T FELT THIS GOOD IN YEARS.
DAMN!
DO YOU KNOW WHAT THIS IS ABOUT?
I HAVE AN IDEA.
CAN I HAVE SOME?
WE'RE HERE.
IVY... WHERE'S YOUR PLANE?
YOU'RE LOOKING AT IT.

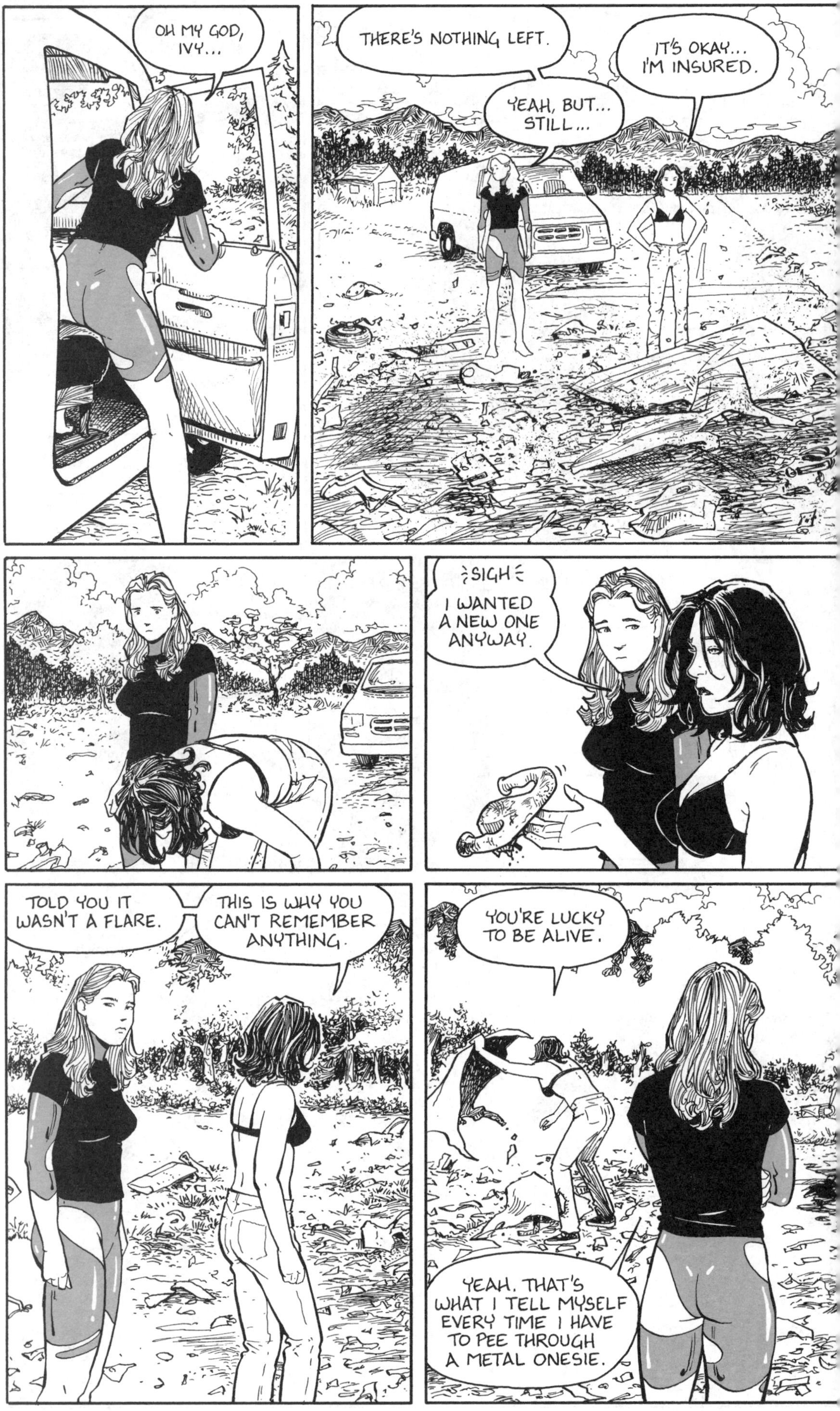

OH MY GOD, IVY...
THERE'S NOTHING LEFT.
YEAH, BUT... STILL...
IT'S OKAY... I'M INSURED.
SIGH
I WANTED A NEW ONE ANYWAY.
TOLD YOU IT WASN'T A FLARE.
THIS IS WHY YOU CAN'T REMEMBER ANYTHING.
YOU'RE LUCKY TO BE ALIVE.
YEAH. THAT'S WHAT I TELL MYSELF EVERY TIME I HAVE TO PEE THROUGH A METAL ONESIE.

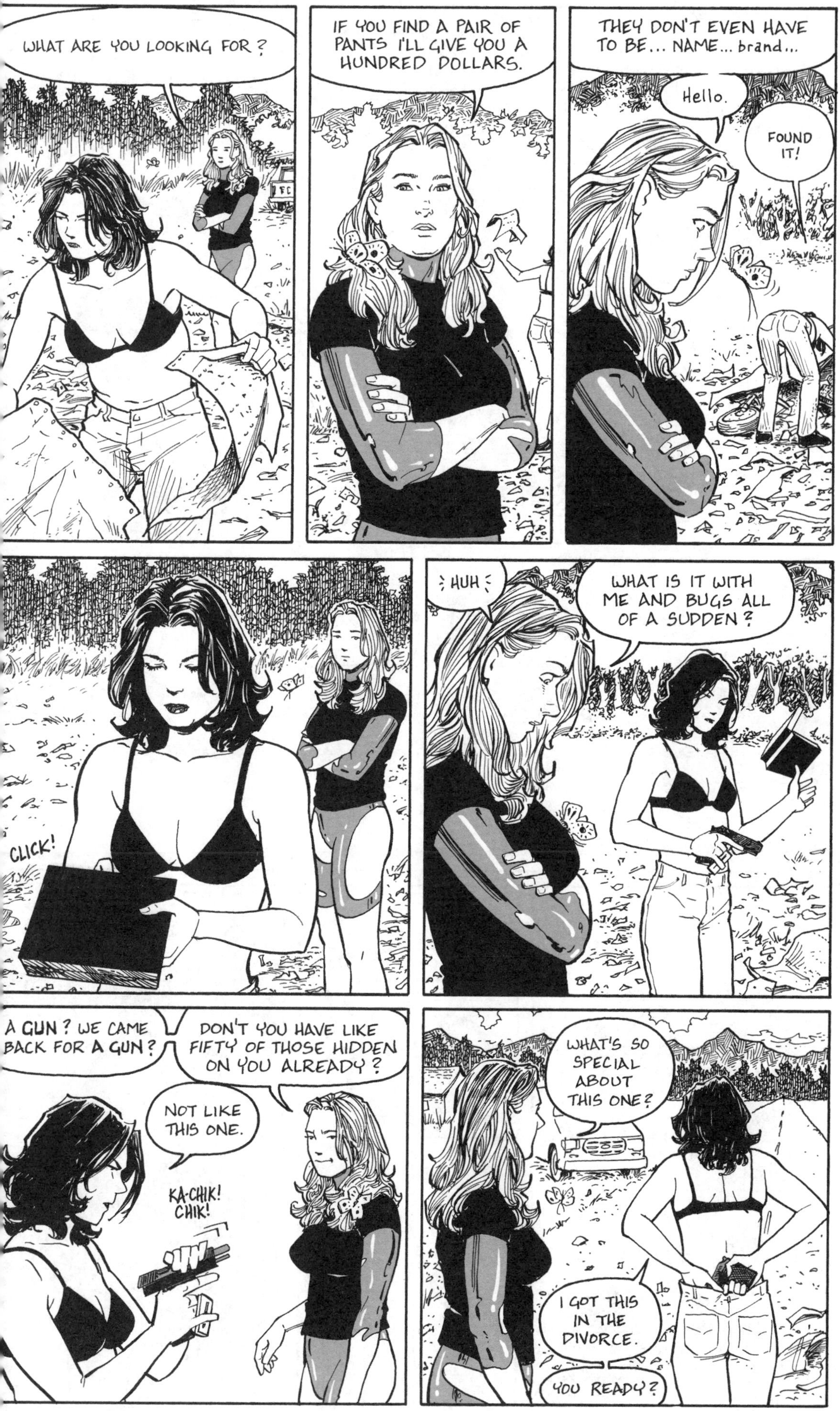
WHAT ARE YOU LOOKING FOR?
IF YOU FIND A PAIR OF PANTS I'LL GIVE YOU A HUNDRED DOLLARS.
THEY DON'T EVEN HAVE TO BE... NAME... brand...
Hello.
FOUND IT!
CLICK!
HUH
WHAT IS IT WITH ME AND BUGS ALL OF A SUDDEN?
A GUN? WE CAME BACK FOR A GUN?
DON'T YOU HAVE LIKE FIFTY OF THOSE HIDDEN ON YOU ALREADY?
NOT LIKE THIS ONE.
KA-CHIK! CHIK!
WHAT'S SO SPECIAL ABOUT THIS ONE?
I GOT THIS IN THE DIVORCE.
YOU READY?

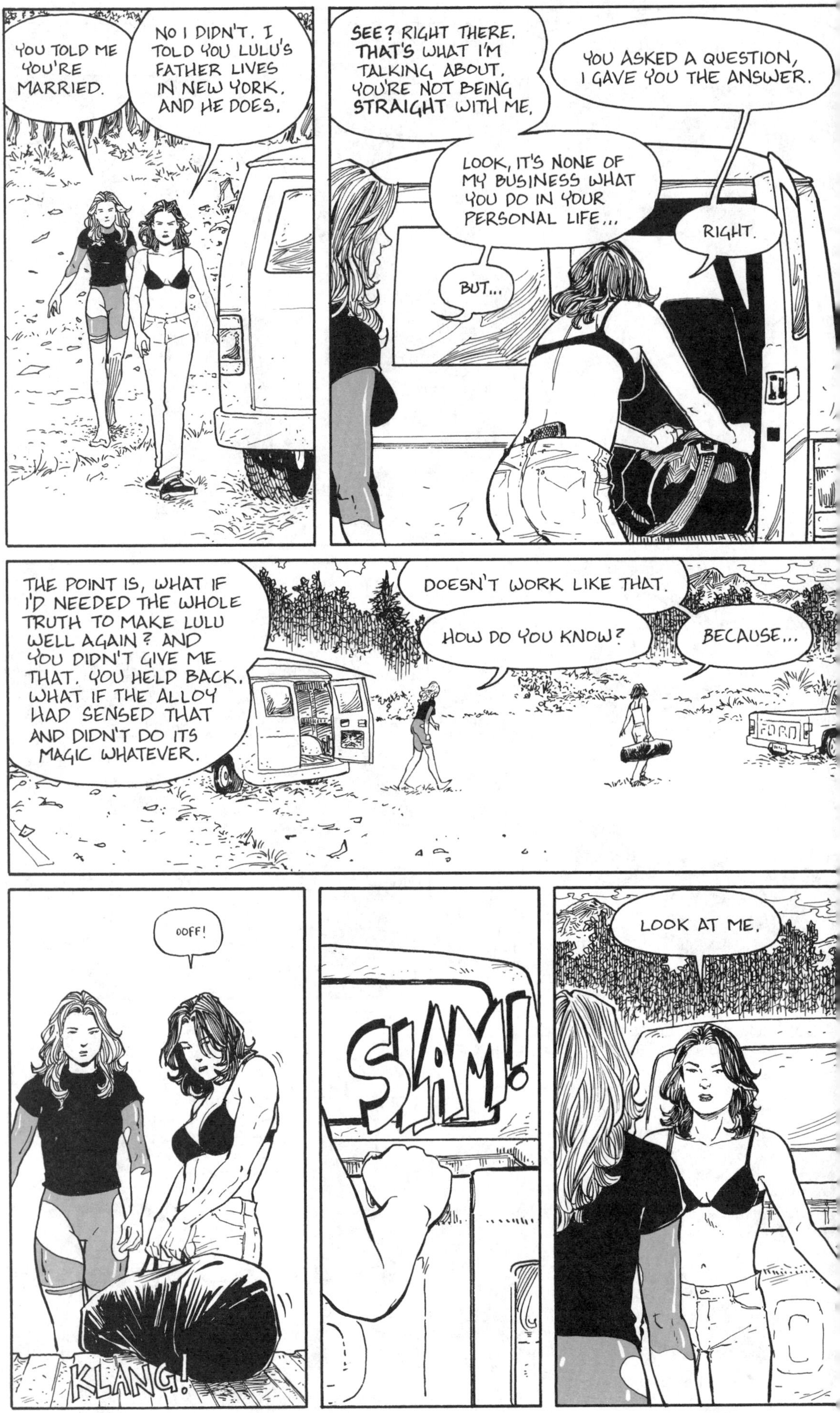
YOU TOLD ME YOU'RE MARRIED.
NO I DIDN'T. I TOLD YOU LULU'S FATHER LIVES IN NEW YORK. AND HE DOES.
SEE? RIGHT THERE. THAT'S WHAT I'M TALKING ABOUT. YOU'RE NOT BEING STRAIGHT WITH ME.
YOU ASKED A QUESTION, I GAVE YOU THE ANSWER.
LOOK, IT'S NONE OF MY BUSINESS WHAT YOU DO IN YOUR PERSONAL LIFE...
RIGHT.
BUT...
THE POINT IS, WHAT IF I'D NEEDED THE WHOLE TRUTH TO MAKE LULU WELL AGAIN? AND YOU DIDN'T GIVE ME THAT. YOU HELD BACK. WHAT IF THE ALLOY HAD SENSED THAT AND DIDN'T DO ITS MAGIC WHATEVER.
DOESN'T WORK LIKE THAT.
HOW DO YOU KNOW?
BECAUSE...
OOFF!
KLANG!
SLAM!
LOOK AT ME.

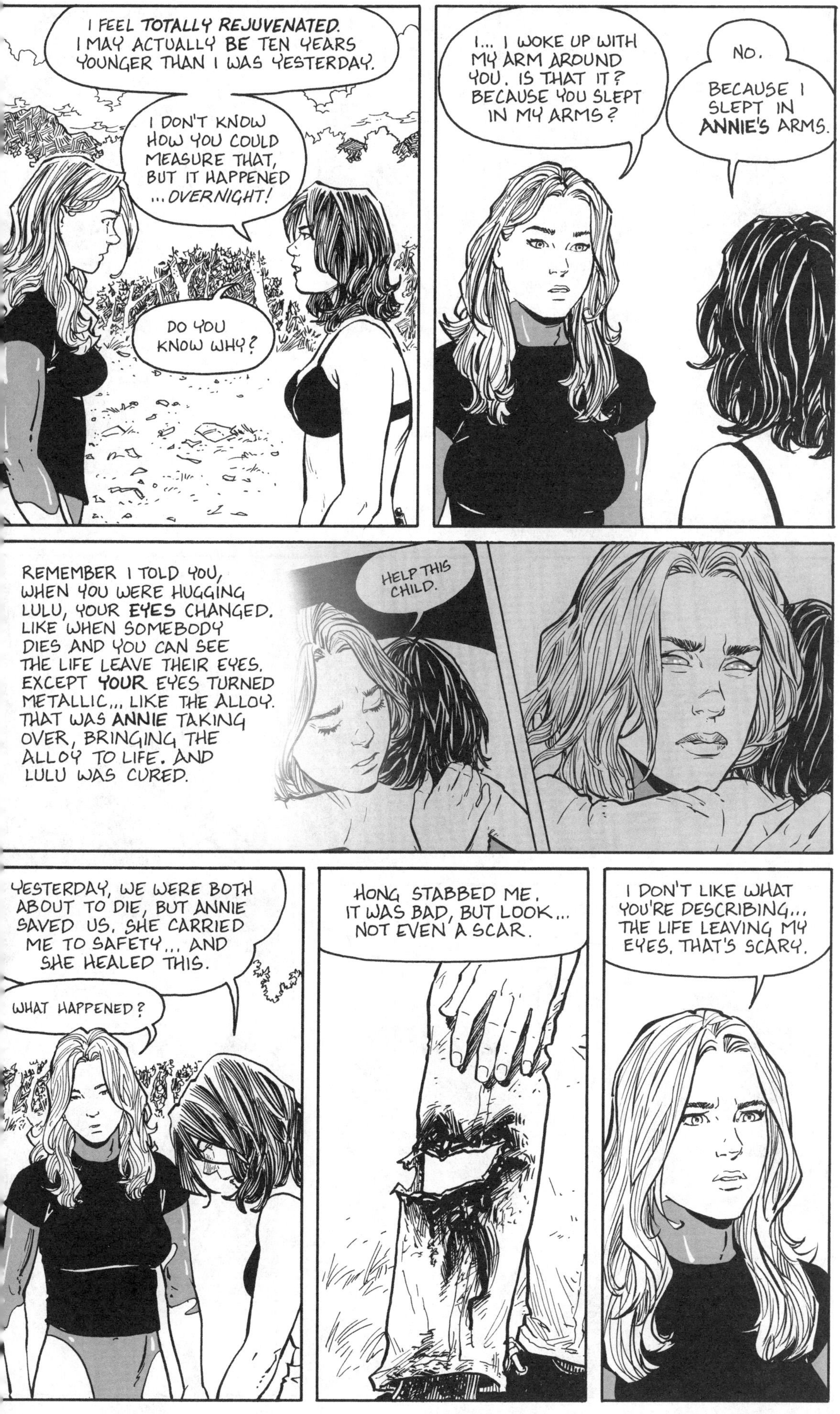
I FEEL TOTALLY REJUVENATED. I MAY ACTUALLY BE TEN YEARS YOUNGER THAN I WAS YESTERDAY.
I DON'T KNOW HOW YOU COULD MEASURE THAT, BUT IT HAPPENED ...OVERNIGHT!
DO YOU KNOW WHY?
I... I WOKE UP WITH MY ARM AROUND YOU. IS THAT IT? BECAUSE YOU SLEPT IN MY ARMS?
NO.
BECAUSE I SLEPT IN ANNIE'S ARMS.
REMEMBER I TOLD YOU, WHEN YOU WERE HUGGING LULU, YOUR EYES CHANGED. LIKE WHEN SOMEBODY DIES AND YOU CAN SEE THE LIFE LEAVE THEIR EYES. EXCEPT YOUR EYES TURNED METALLIC... LIKE THE ALLOY. THAT WAS ANNIE TAKING OVER, BRINGING THE ALLOY TO LIFE. AND LULU WAS CURED.
HELP THIS CHILD.
YESTERDAY, WE WERE BOTH ABOUT TO DIE, BUT ANNIE SAVED US. SHE CARRIED ME TO SAFETY... AND SHE HEALED THIS.
WHAT HAPPENED?
HONG STABBED ME. IT WAS BAD, BUT LOOK... NOT EVEN A SCAR.
I DON'T LIKE WHAT YOU'RE DESCRIBING... THE LIFE LEAVING MY EYES. THAT'S SCARY.

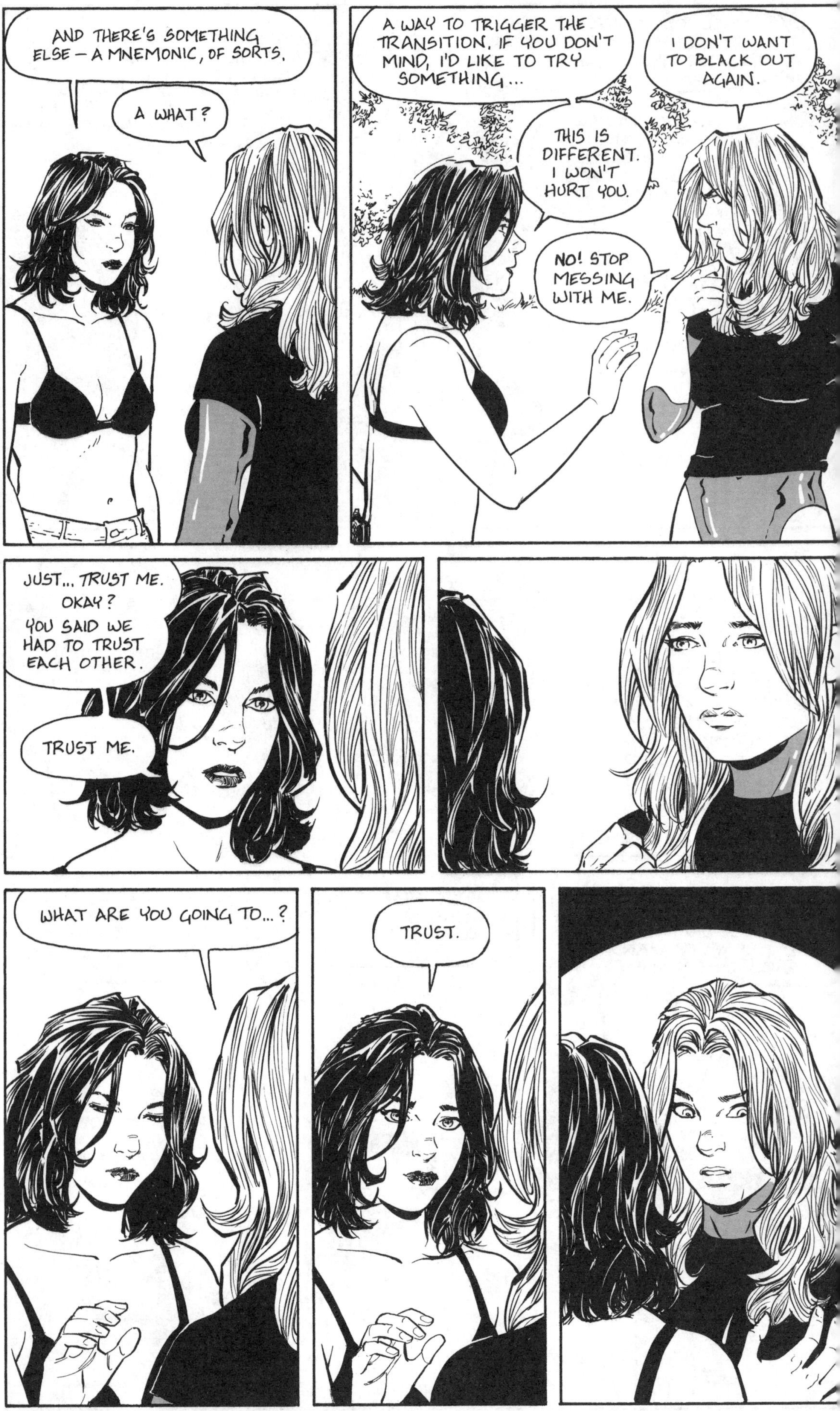

AND THERE'S SOMETHING ELSE — A MNEMONIC, OF SORTS.
A WHAT?
A WAY TO TRIGGER THE TRANSITION. IF YOU DON'T MIND, I'D LIKE TO TRY SOMETHING...
I DON'T WANT TO BLACK OUT AGAIN.
THIS IS DIFFERENT. I WON'T HURT YOU.
NO! STOP MESSING WITH ME.
JUST... TRUST ME. OKAY? YOU SAID WE HAD TO TRUST EACH OTHER.
TRUST ME.
WHAT ARE YOU GOING TO...?
TRUST.

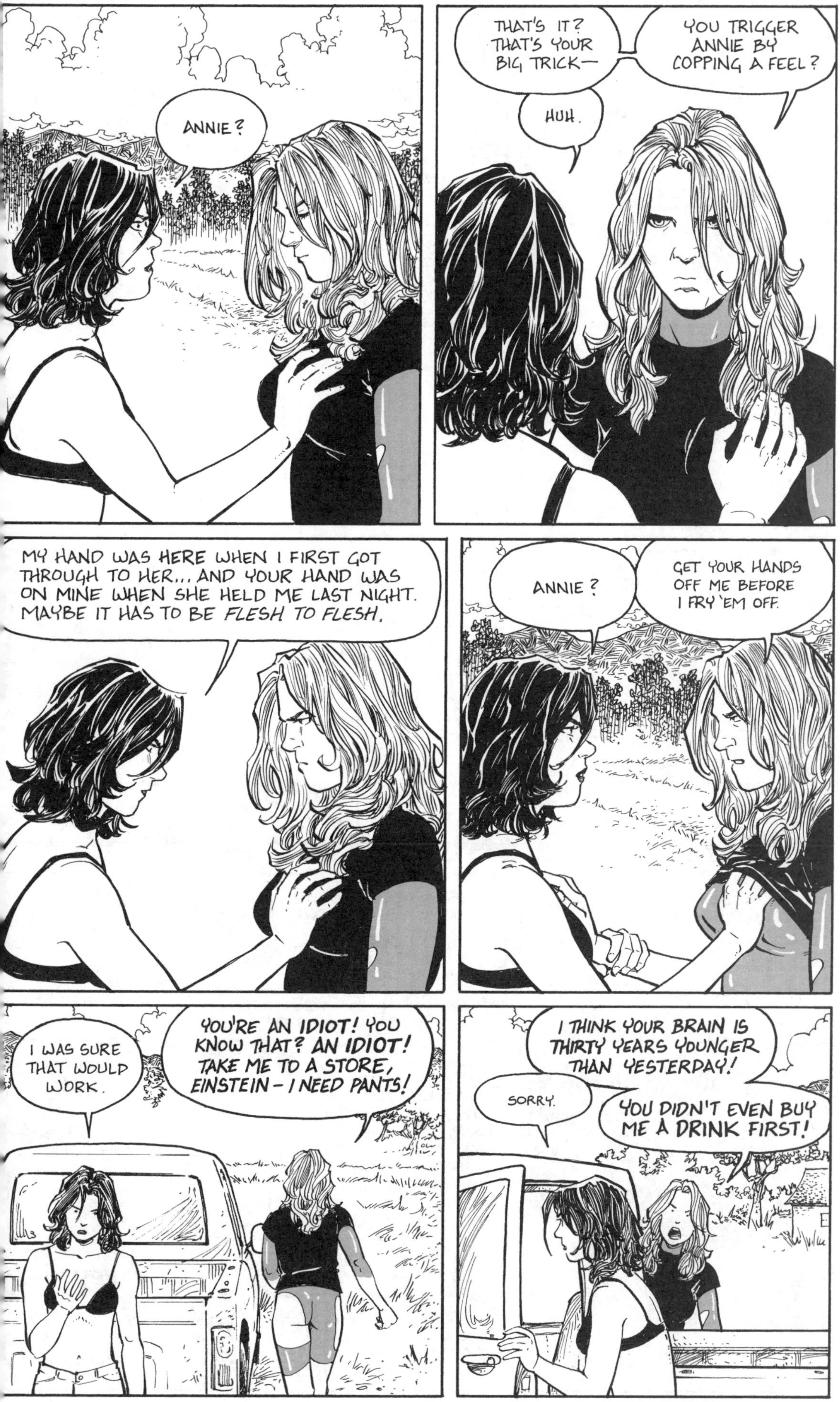
ANNIE?
THAT'S IT? THAT'S YOUR BIG TRICK—
YOU TRIGGER ANNIE BY COPPING A FEEL?
HUH.
MY HAND WAS HERE WHEN I FIRST GOT THROUGH TO HER... AND YOUR HAND WAS ON MINE WHEN SHE HELD ME LAST NIGHT. MAYBE IT HAS TO BE *FLESH TO FLESH*.
ANNIE?
GET YOUR HANDS OFF ME BEFORE I FRY 'EM OFF.
I WAS SURE THAT WOULD WORK.
YOU'RE AN **IDIOT**! YOU KNOW THAT? **AN IDIOT**! TAKE ME TO A STORE, EINSTEIN – I NEED PANTS!
I THINK YOUR BRAIN IS THIRTY YEARS YOUNGER THAN YESTERDAY!
SORRY.
YOU DIDN'T EVEN BUY ME A DRINK FIRST!

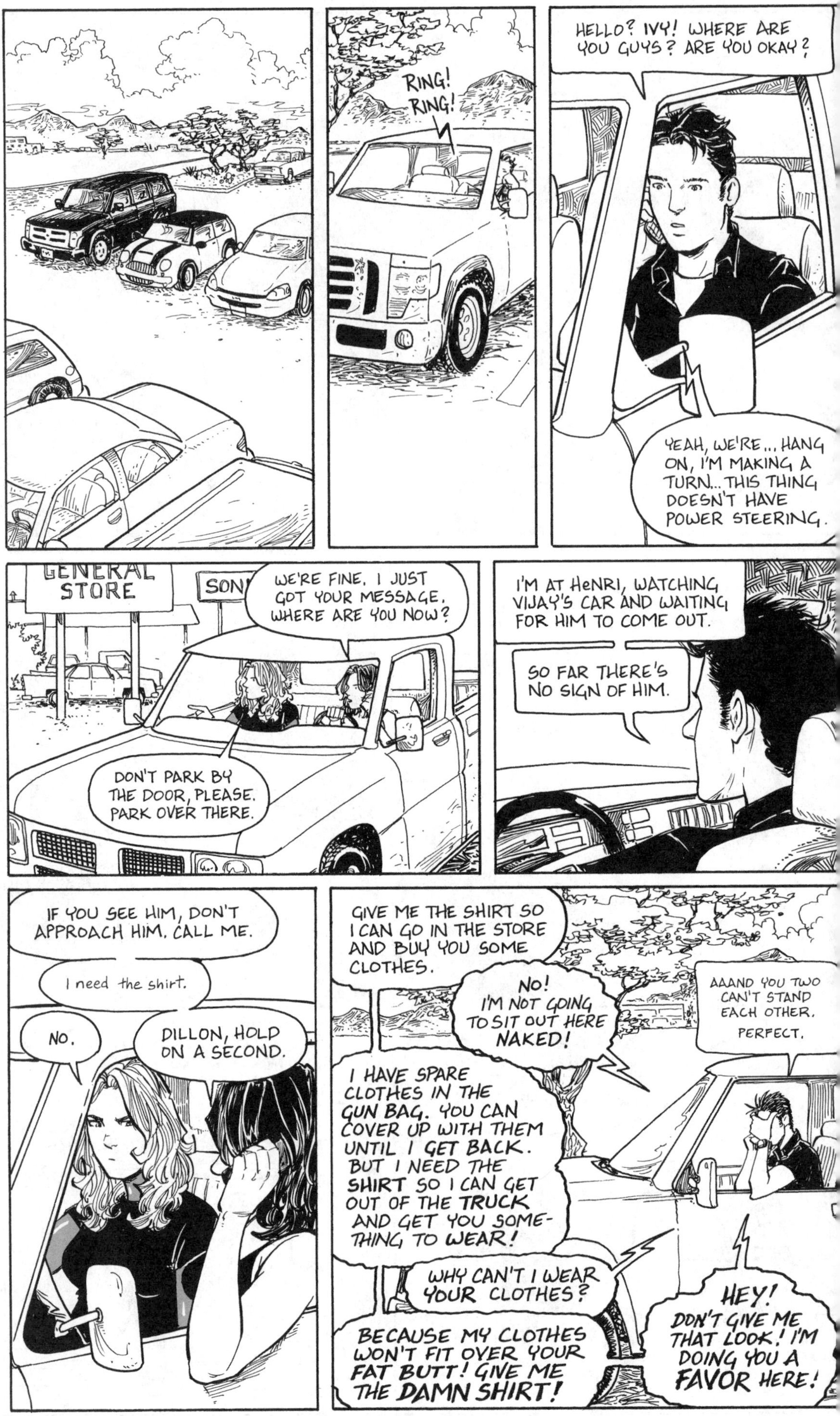
RING! RING!
HELLO? IVY! WHERE ARE YOU GUYS? ARE YOU OKAY?
YEAH, WE'RE... HANG ON, I'M MAKING A TURN... THIS THING DOESN'T HAVE POWER STEERING.
GENERAL STORE
WE'RE FINE. I JUST GOT YOUR MESSAGE. WHERE ARE YOU NOW?
DON'T PARK BY THE DOOR, PLEASE. PARK OVER THERE.
I'M AT HeNRI, WATCHING VIJAY'S CAR AND WAITING FOR HIM TO COME OUT.
SO FAR THERE'S NO SIGN OF HIM.
IF YOU SEE HIM, DON'T APPROACH HIM. CALL ME.
I need the shirt.
NO.
DILLON, HOLD ON A SECOND.
GIVE ME THE SHIRT SO I CAN GO IN THE STORE AND BUY YOU SOME CLOTHES.
NO! I'M NOT GOING TO SIT OUT HERE NAKED!
I HAVE SPARE CLOTHES IN THE GUN BAG. YOU CAN COVER UP WITH THEM UNTIL I GET BACK. BUT I NEED THE SHIRT SO I CAN GET OUT OF THE TRUCK AND GET YOU SOMETHING TO WEAR!
WHY CAN'T I WEAR YOUR CLOTHES?
BECAUSE MY CLOTHES WON'T FIT OVER YOUR FAT BUTT! GIVE ME THE DAMN SHIRT!
AAAND YOU TWO CAN'T STAND EACH OTHER. PERFECT.
HEY! DON'T GIVE ME THAT LOOK! I'M DOING YOU A FAVOR HERE!

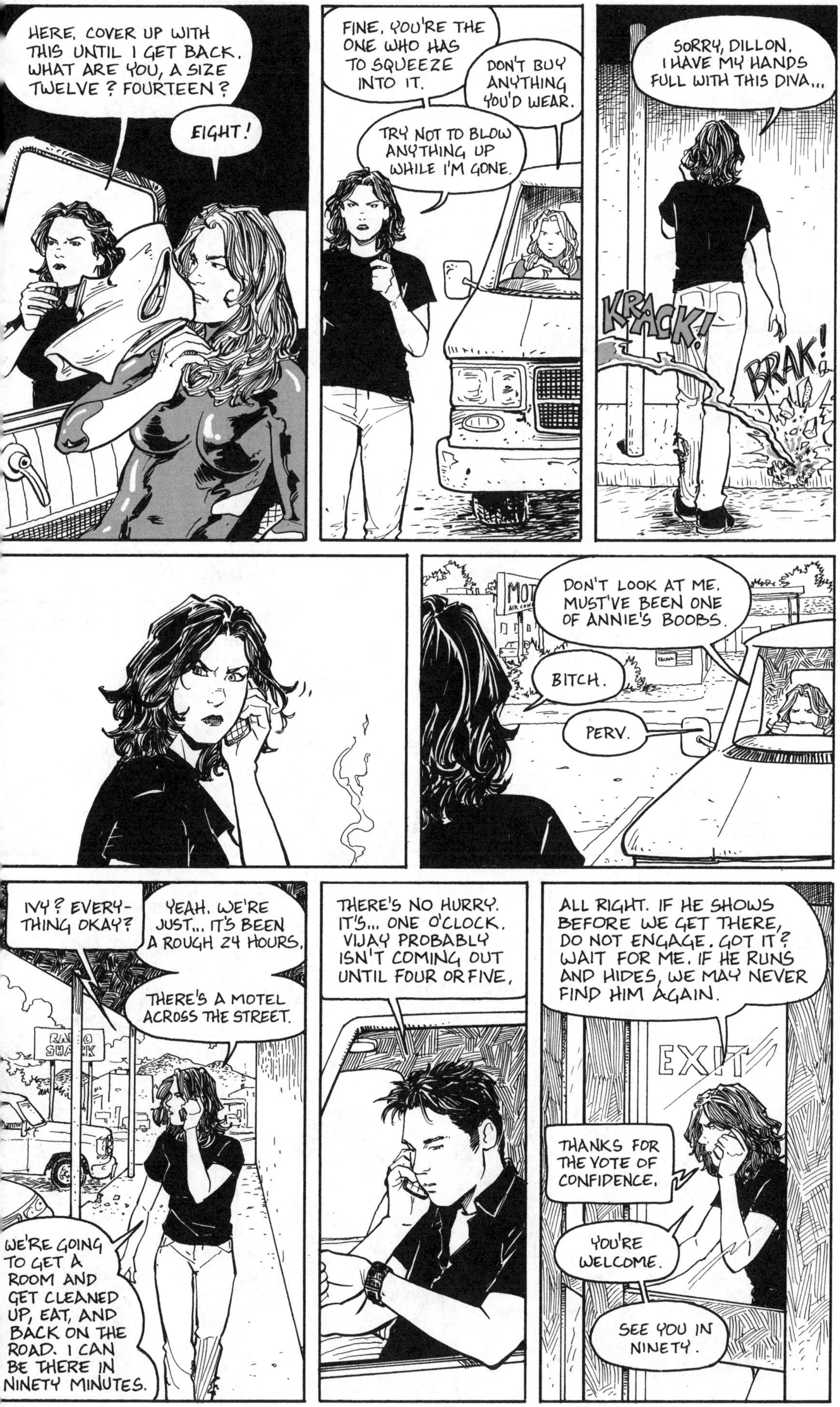
HERE, COVER UP WITH THIS UNTIL I GET BACK. WHAT ARE YOU, A SIZE TWELVE? FOURTEEN?
EIGHT!
FINE. YOU'RE THE ONE WHO HAS TO SQUEEZE INTO IT.
DON'T BUY ANYTHING YOU'D WEAR.
TRY NOT TO BLOW ANYTHING UP WHILE I'M GONE.
SORRY, DILLON. I HAVE MY HANDS FULL WITH THIS DIVA...
KRACK!
BRAK!
DON'T LOOK AT ME. MUST'VE BEEN ONE OF ANNIE'S BOOBS.
BITCH.
PERV.
IVY? EVERYTHING OKAY?
YEAH. WE'RE JUST... IT'S BEEN A ROUGH 24 HOURS.
THERE'S A MOTEL ACROSS THE STREET.
WE'RE GOING TO GET A ROOM AND GET CLEANED UP, EAT, AND BACK ON THE ROAD. I CAN BE THERE IN NINETY MINUTES.
THERE'S NO HURRY. IT'S... ONE O'CLOCK. VIJAY PROBABLY ISN'T COMING OUT UNTIL FOUR OR FIVE.
ALL RIGHT. IF HE SHOWS BEFORE WE GET THERE, DO NOT ENGAGE. GOT IT? WAIT FOR ME. IF HE RUNS AND HIDES, WE MAY NEVER FIND HIM AGAIN.
EXIT
THANKS FOR THE VOTE OF CONFIDENCE.
YOU'RE WELCOME.
SEE YOU IN NINETY.

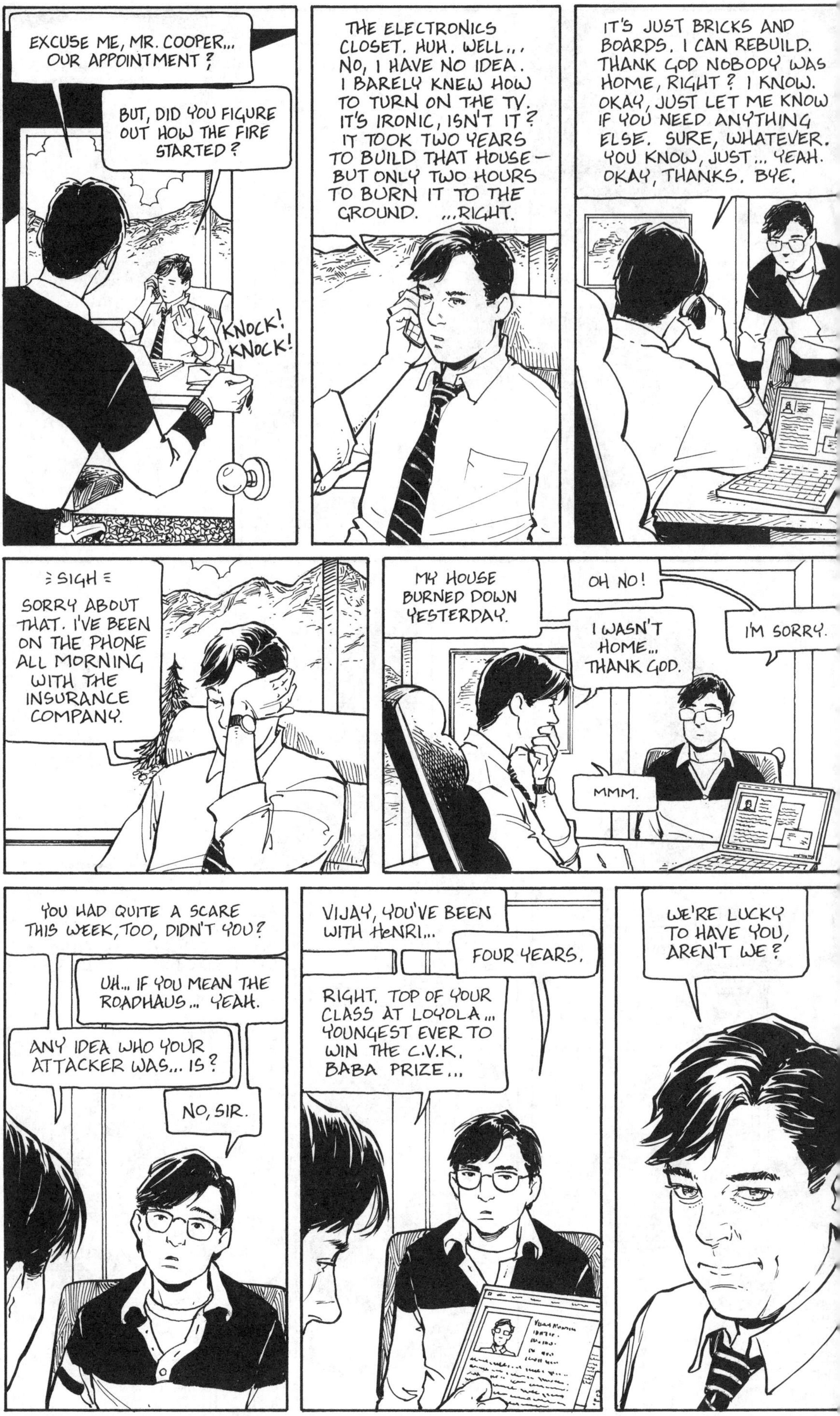
EXCUSE ME, MR. COOPER... OUR APPOINTMENT?
BUT, DID YOU FIGURE OUT HOW THE FIRE STARTED?
KNOCK! KNOCK!
THE ELECTRONICS CLOSET. HUH. WELL... NO, I HAVE NO IDEA. I BARELY KNEW HOW TO TURN ON THE TV. IT'S IRONIC, ISN'T IT? IT TOOK TWO YEARS TO BUILD THAT HOUSE— BUT ONLY TWO HOURS TO BURN IT TO THE GROUND. ...RIGHT.
IT'S JUST BRICKS AND BOARDS. I CAN REBUILD. THANK GOD NOBODY WAS HOME, RIGHT? I KNOW. OKAY, JUST LET ME KNOW IF YOU NEED ANYTHING ELSE. SURE, WHATEVER. YOU KNOW, JUST... YEAH. OKAY, THANKS. BYE.
SIGH
SORRY ABOUT THAT. I'VE BEEN ON THE PHONE ALL MORNING WITH THE INSURANCE COMPANY.
MY HOUSE BURNED DOWN YESTERDAY.
OH NO!
I WASN'T HOME... THANK GOD.
I'M SORRY.
MMM.
YOU HAD QUITE A SCARE THIS WEEK, TOO, DIDN'T YOU?
UH... IF YOU MEAN THE ROADHAUS... YEAH.
ANY IDEA WHO YOUR ATTACKER WAS... IS?
NO, SIR.
VIJAY, YOU'VE BEEN WITH HeNRI...
FOUR YEARS.
RIGHT. TOP OF YOUR CLASS AT LOYOLA... YOUNGEST EVER TO WIN THE C.V.K. BABA PRIZE...
WE'RE LUCKY TO HAVE YOU, AREN'T WE?

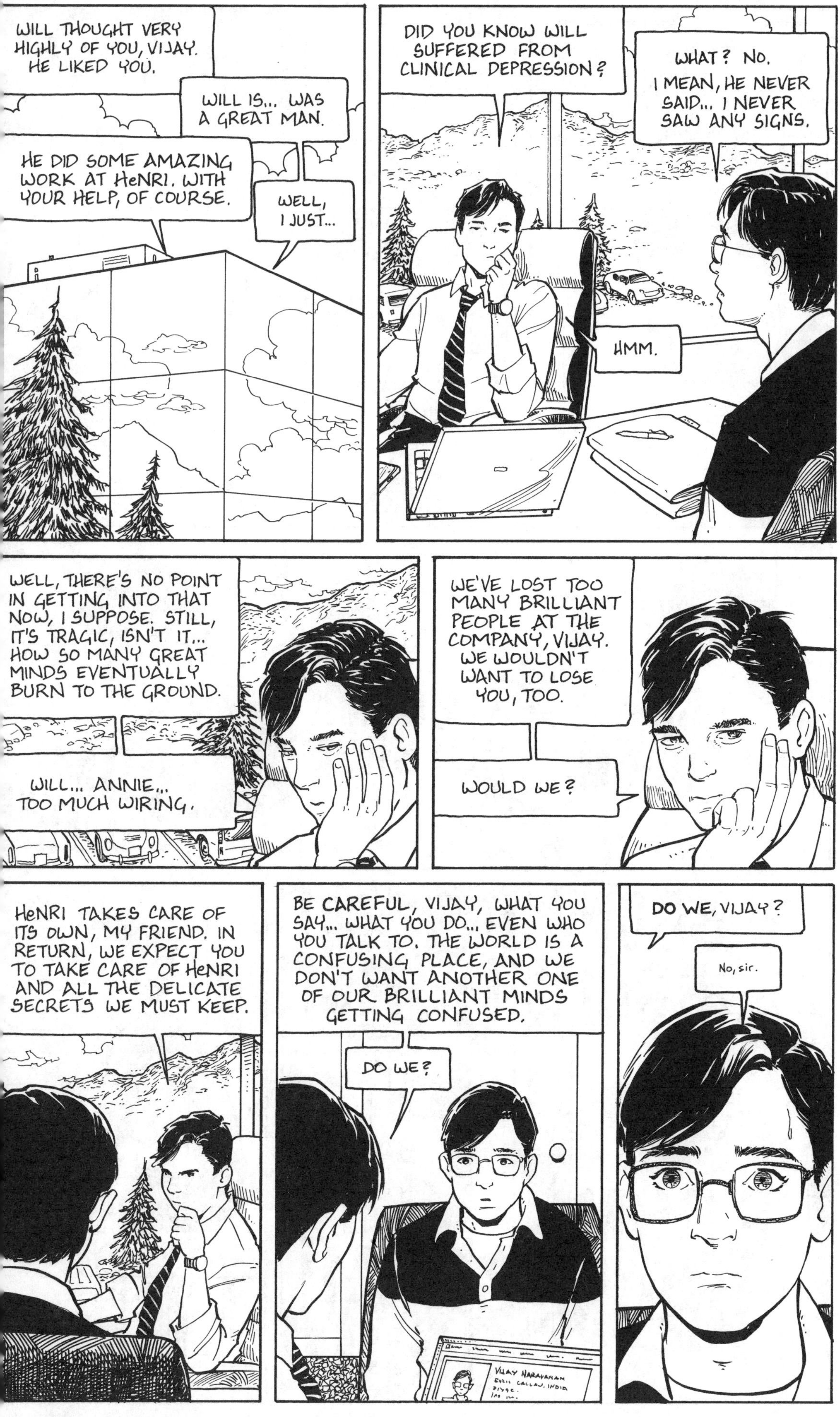
WILL THOUGHT VERY HIGHLY OF YOU, VIJAY. HE LIKED YOU.
WILL IS... WAS A GREAT MAN.
HE DID SOME AMAZING WORK AT HeNRI. WITH YOUR HELP, OF COURSE.
WELL, I JUST...
DID YOU KNOW WILL SUFFERED FROM CLINICAL DEPRESSION?
WHAT? NO.
I MEAN, HE NEVER SAID... I NEVER SAW ANY SIGNS.
HMM.
WELL, THERE'S NO POINT IN GETTING INTO THAT NOW, I SUPPOSE. STILL, IT'S TRAGIC, ISN'T IT... HOW SO MANY GREAT MINDS EVENTUALLY BURN TO THE GROUND.
WILL... ANNIE... TOO MUCH WIRING.
WE'VE LOST TOO MANY BRILLIANT PEOPLE AT THE COMPANY, VIJAY. WE WOULDN'T WANT TO LOSE YOU, TOO.
WOULD WE?
HeNRI TAKES CARE OF ITS OWN, MY FRIEND. IN RETURN, WE EXPECT YOU TO TAKE CARE OF HeNRI AND ALL THE DELICATE SECRETS WE MUST KEEP.
BE CAREFUL, VIJAY, WHAT YOU SAY... WHAT YOU DO... EVEN WHO YOU TALK TO. THE WORLD IS A CONFUSING PLACE, AND WE DON'T WANT ANOTHER ONE OF OUR BRILLIANT MINDS GETTING CONFUSED.
DO WE?
VIJAY NARAYANAN
DO WE, VIJAY?
No, sir.

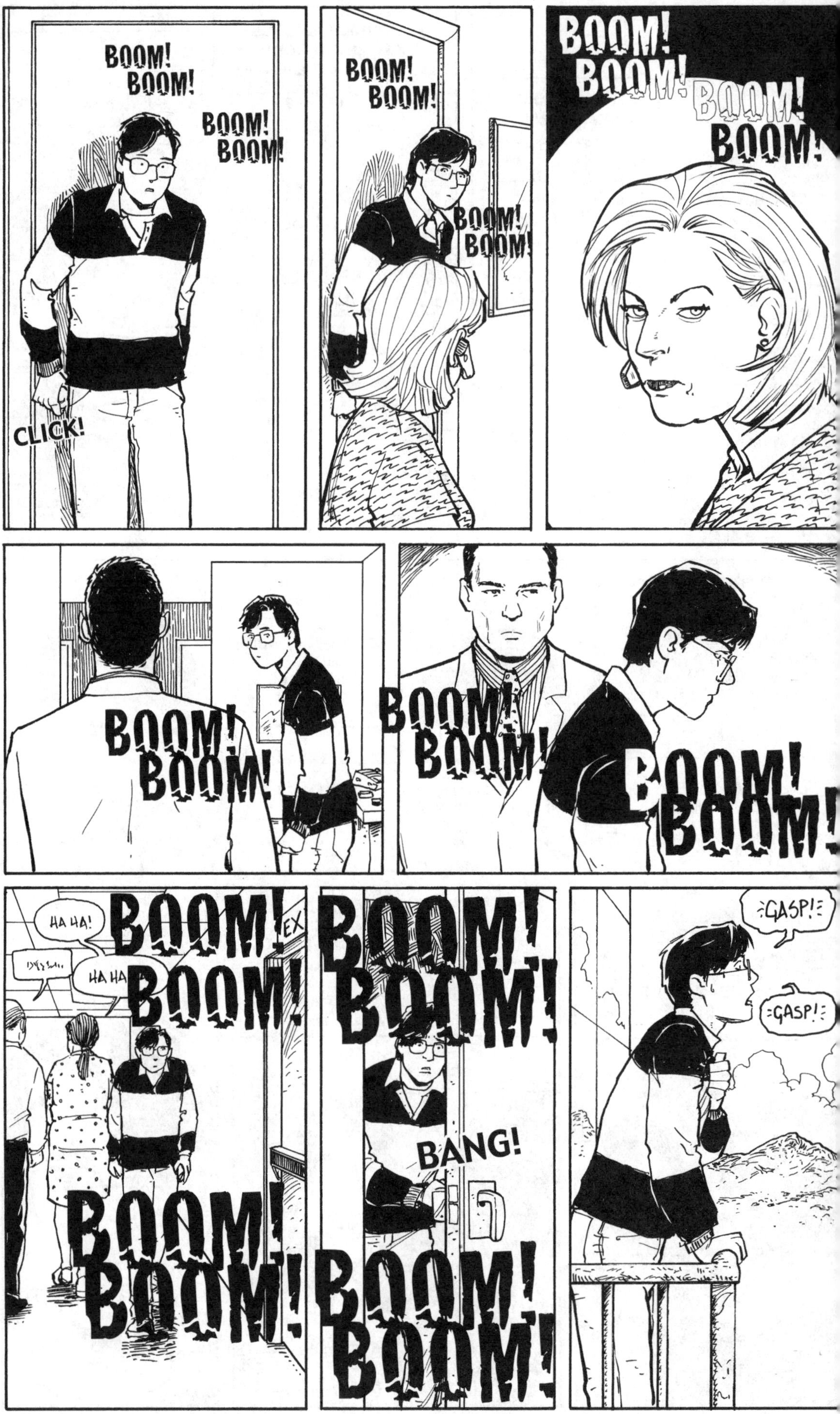

BOOM!
BOOM!
BOOM!
BOOM!
CLICK!
BOOM!
BOOM!
BOOM!
BOOM!
BOOM!
BOOM!
BOOM!
BOOM!
BOOM!
BOOM!
BOOM!
BOOM!
BOOM!
BOOM!
HA HA!
HA HA
BOOM!
BOOM!
BOOM!
BOOM!
BOOM!
BOOM!
BANG!
BOOM!
BOOM!
GASP!
GASP!

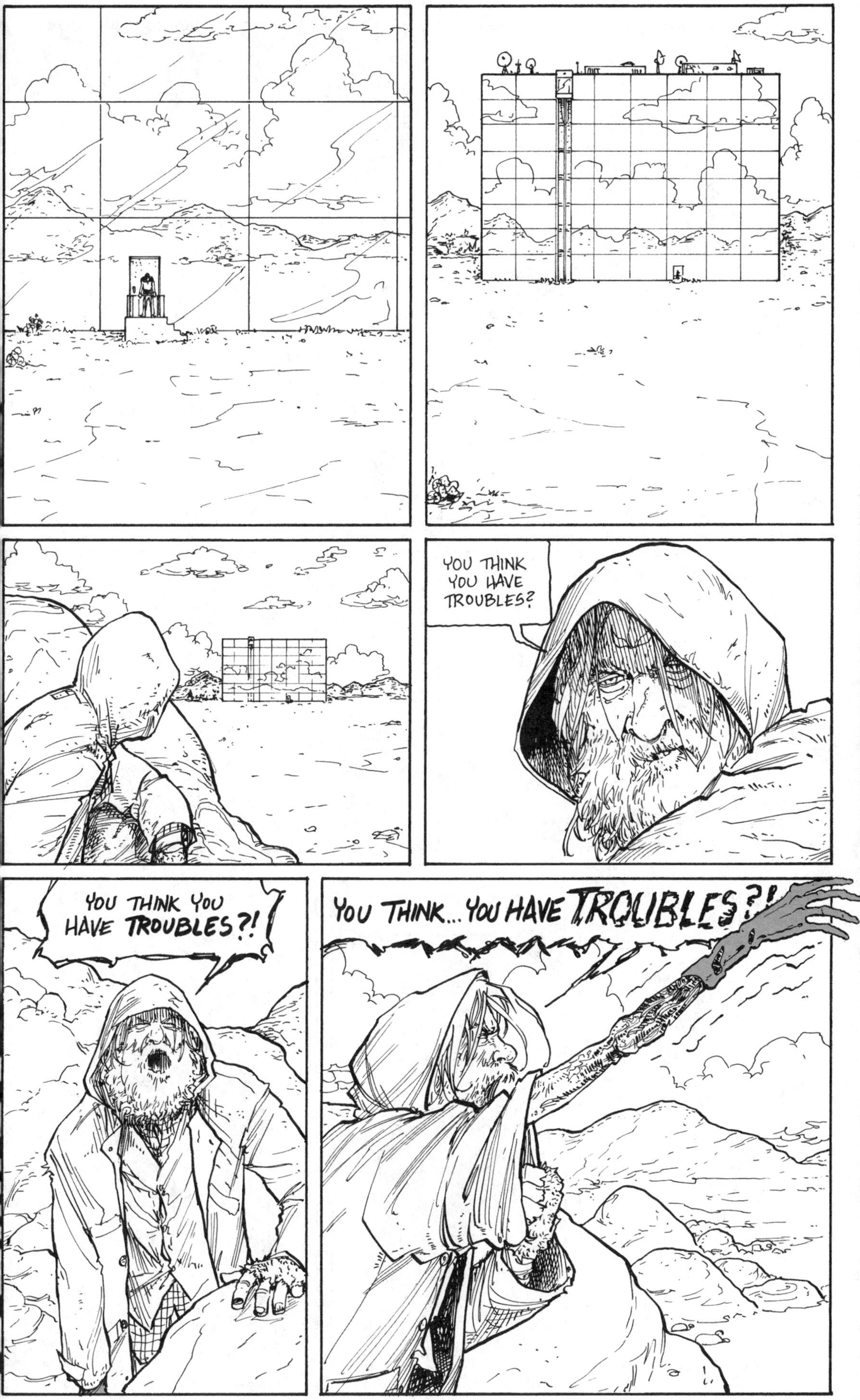
YOU THINK YOU HAVE TROUBLES?
YOU THINK YOU HAVE TROUBLES?!
YOU THINK... YOU HAVE TROUBLES?!

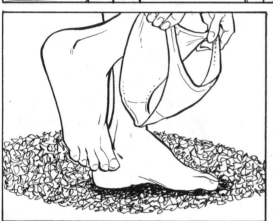

CRAP.

THIS UNDER-WEAR IS TOO SMALL.

AND I CAN ALREADY TELL THESE ARE NOT SIZE 8.

DAMMIT, IVY!

WHAT ARE YOU YELLING ABOUT NOW?

I TOLD YOU I'M A SIZE 8!

YEAH, AND I TOLD YOU, YOU'RE CRAZY, BUT I BOUGHT 8'S.

THE SHORTS, THE SHIRTS... ALL 8'S.

THERE'S NO WAY THESE ARE SIZE...

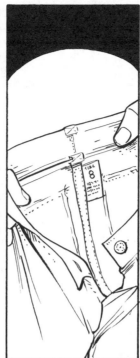

I... I DON'T UNDERSTAND. THIS BRAND MUST RUN SMALL OR...

JULIE...

HOW TALL ARE YOU?

FIVE SEVEN.

REALLY.

YEAH. ON THE DOT. WHY? HOW TALL ARE YOU?

FIVE EIGHT.

I THOUGHT SOMETHING WAS OFF, BUT THE CHANGE WAS SO GRADUAL...

WHAT'S HAPPENING TO ME?

YOU'RE GROWING...

GETTING BIGGER... STRONGER...

WHY?!

"Fear makes the wolf bigger than he is."
— German Proverb

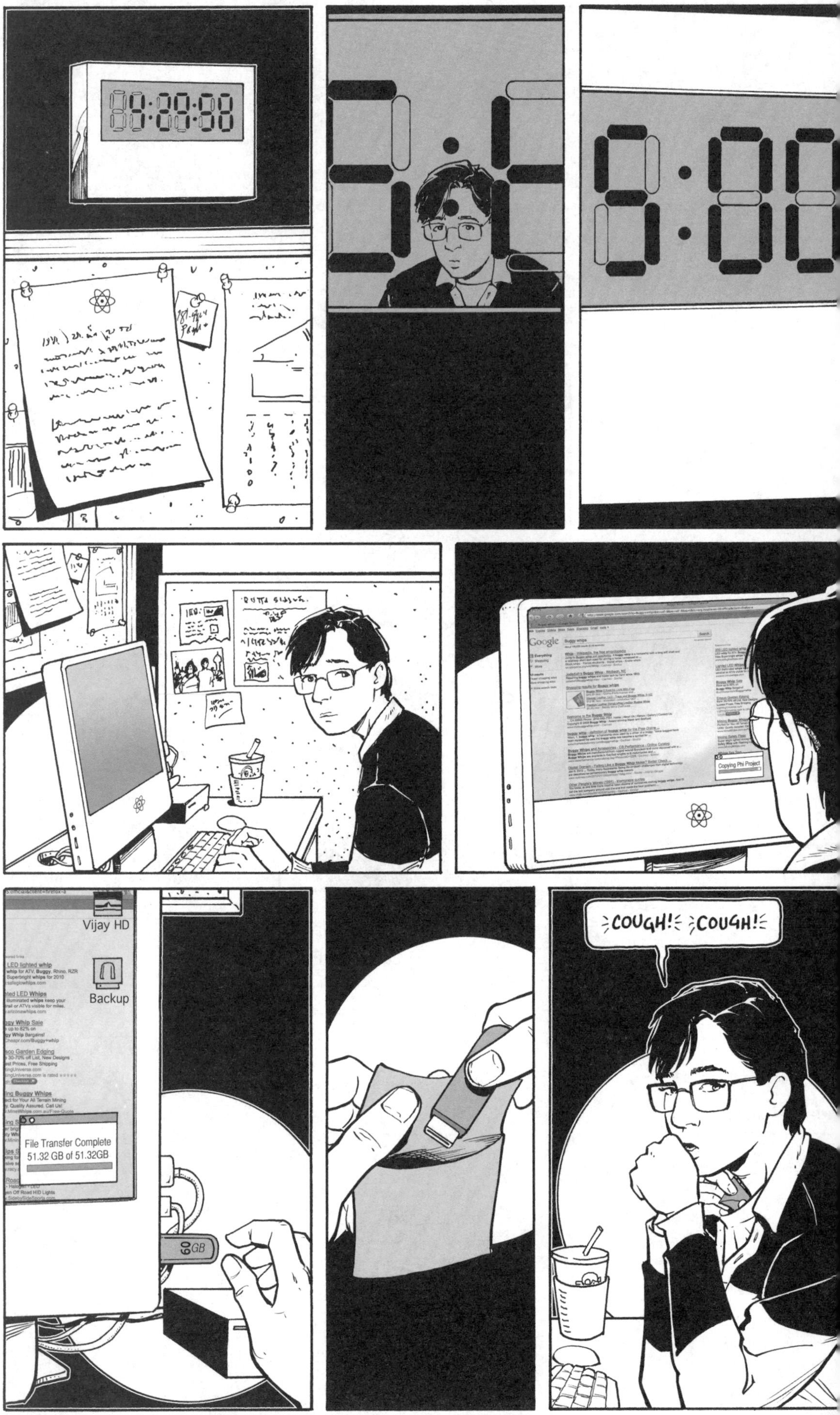
Copying Phi Project
Vijay HD
Backup
File Transfer Complete
51.32 GB of 51.32GB
60GB
COUGH! COUGH!

Vijay HD
Mount Eject Enable Journaling New Image Convert Resize Image
Secure Erase Options
These options specify how to erase the selected disk or volume to prevent
recovery applications from recovering it.
Don't Erase Data
This is quick and provides the least security. It erases just the information use
access your files and leaves the data in the files unchanged. Many commonly
disk recovery applications can restore that data.
Zero Out Data
This is quick and provides good security. It erases the information used to ac
files and writes zeros over the data once.
7-Pass Erase
This option takes 7 times longer than "Zero Out Data," and meets the US Dep
Defense (DOD) 5220-22 M standard for securely erasing magnetic media. It e
information used to access your files and writes over the data 7 times.
35-Pass Erase
This option takes 35 times longer than "Zero Out Data" and provides the best
It erases the information used to access your files and writes over the data 35
Cancel
Mount Point : /
Format : Mac OS Extended (Journaled)
ners Enabled : Yes
er of Folders : 167,479
Capacity : 186.0 GB (199,705,673,728
Available : 109.0 GB (117,078,908,928
Used : 77.0 GB (82,626,764,800 By
Number of Files : 686,976
CLICK!
return
enter
First Aid Erase Partition RAID Restore
Erase option: 35 Pass Secure Erase selected.
Writing zeros to disk. Estimated time: 55 minutes
SEE YOU TOMORROW, VIJAY.
BYE, D.

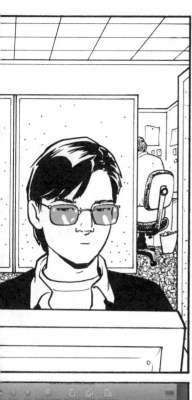

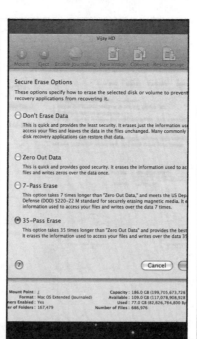

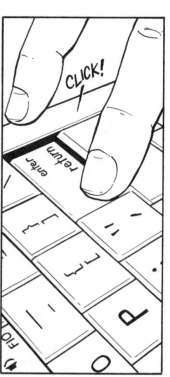

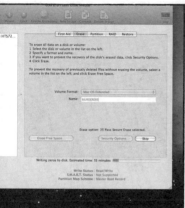

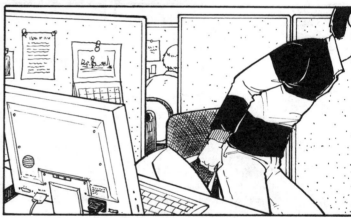

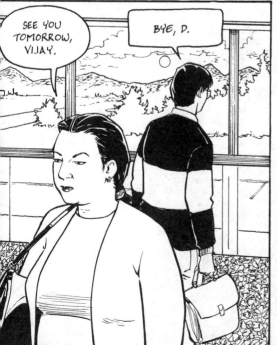

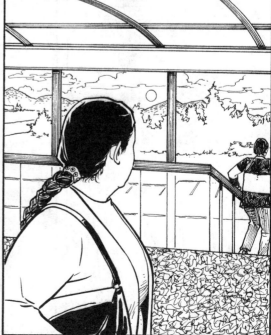

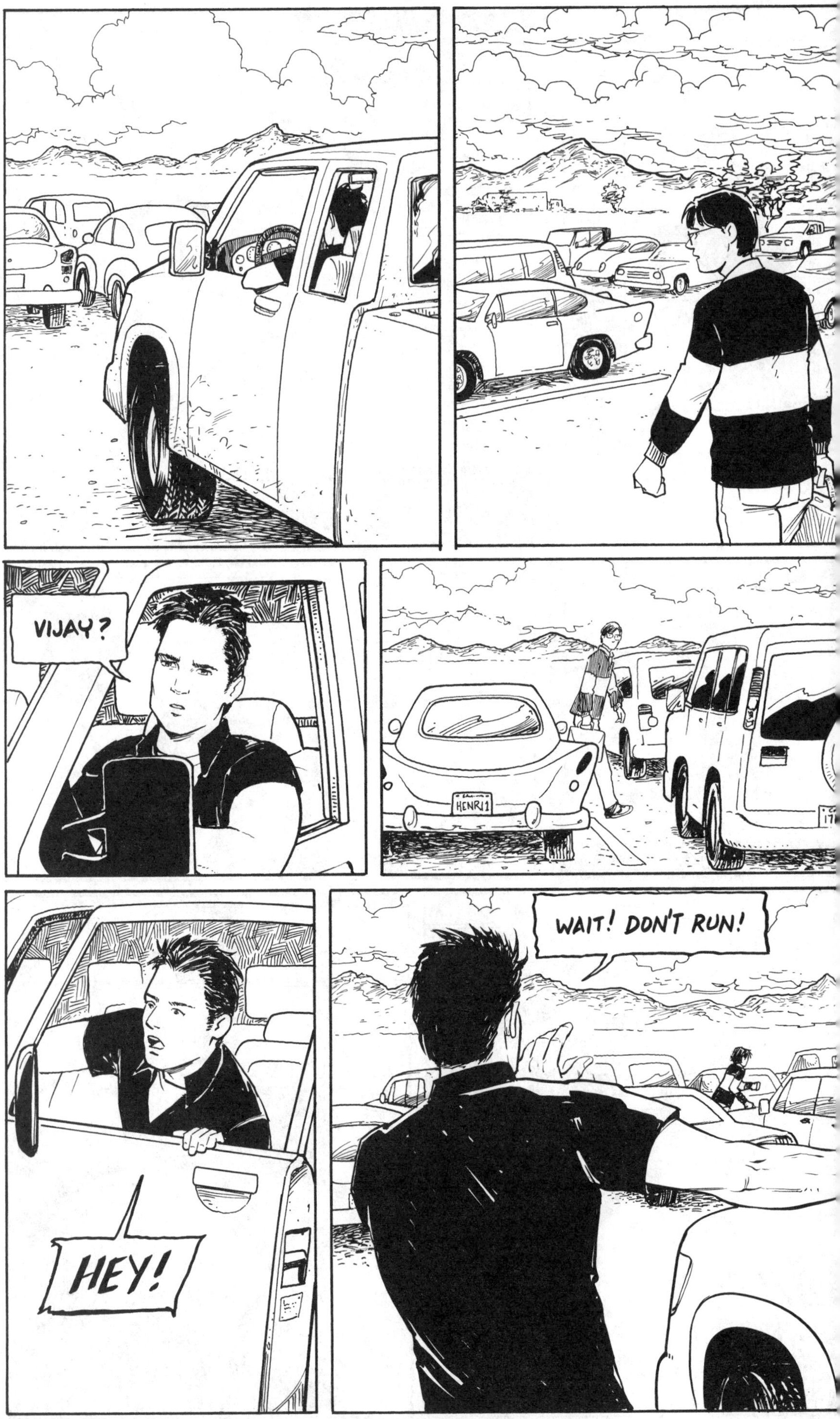
VIJAY?
HENRI 1
HEY!
WAIT! DON'T RUN!

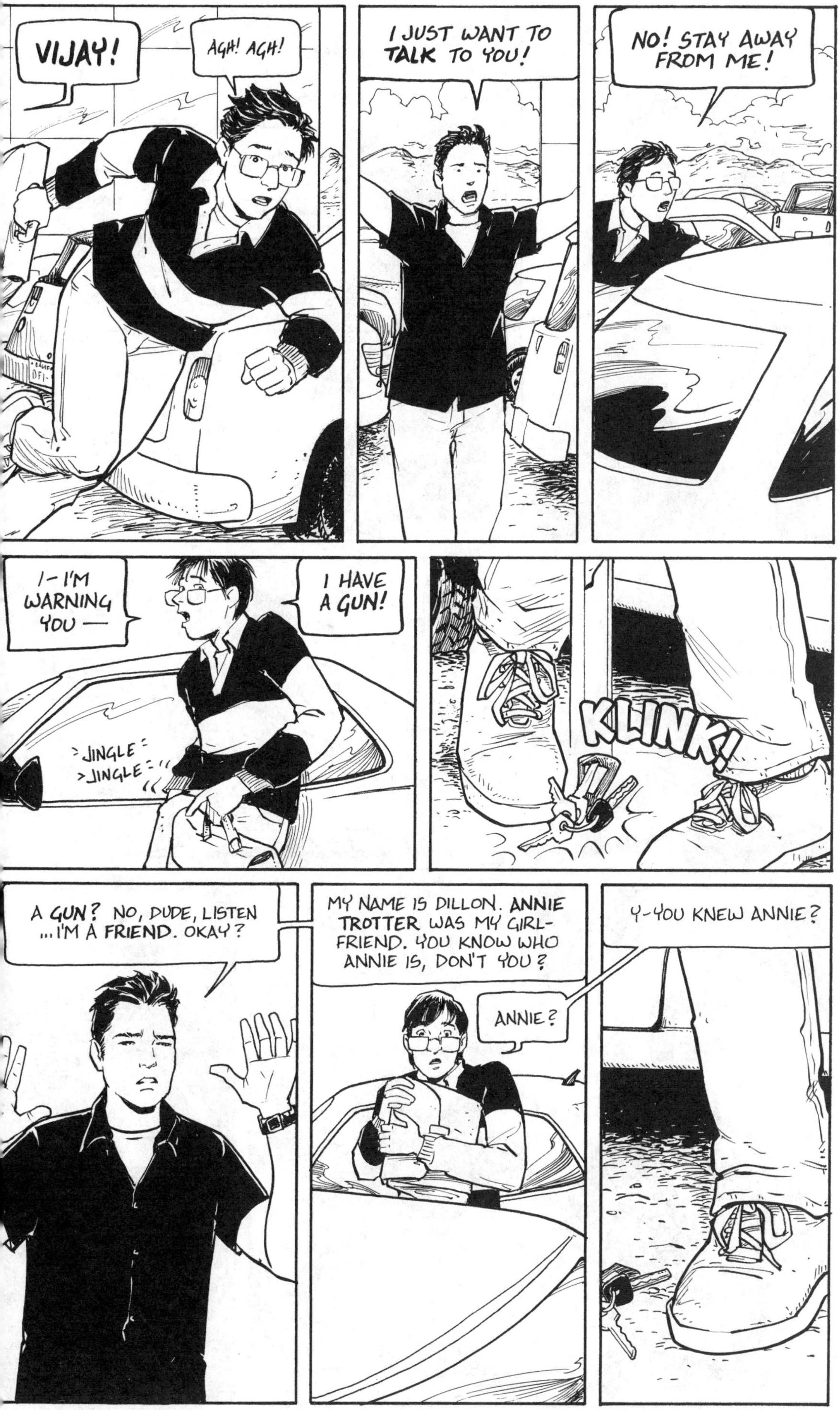
VIJAY!
AGH! AGH!
I JUST WANT TO TALK TO YOU!
NO! STAY AWAY FROM ME!
I- I'M WARNING YOU —
I HAVE A GUN!
JINGLE
JINGLE
KLINK!
A GUN? NO, DUDE, LISTEN ...I'M A FRIEND. OKAY?
MY NAME IS DILLON. ANNIE TROTTER WAS MY GIRL-FRIEND. YOU KNOW WHO ANNIE IS, DON'T YOU?
ANNIE?
Y-YOU KNEW ANNIE?

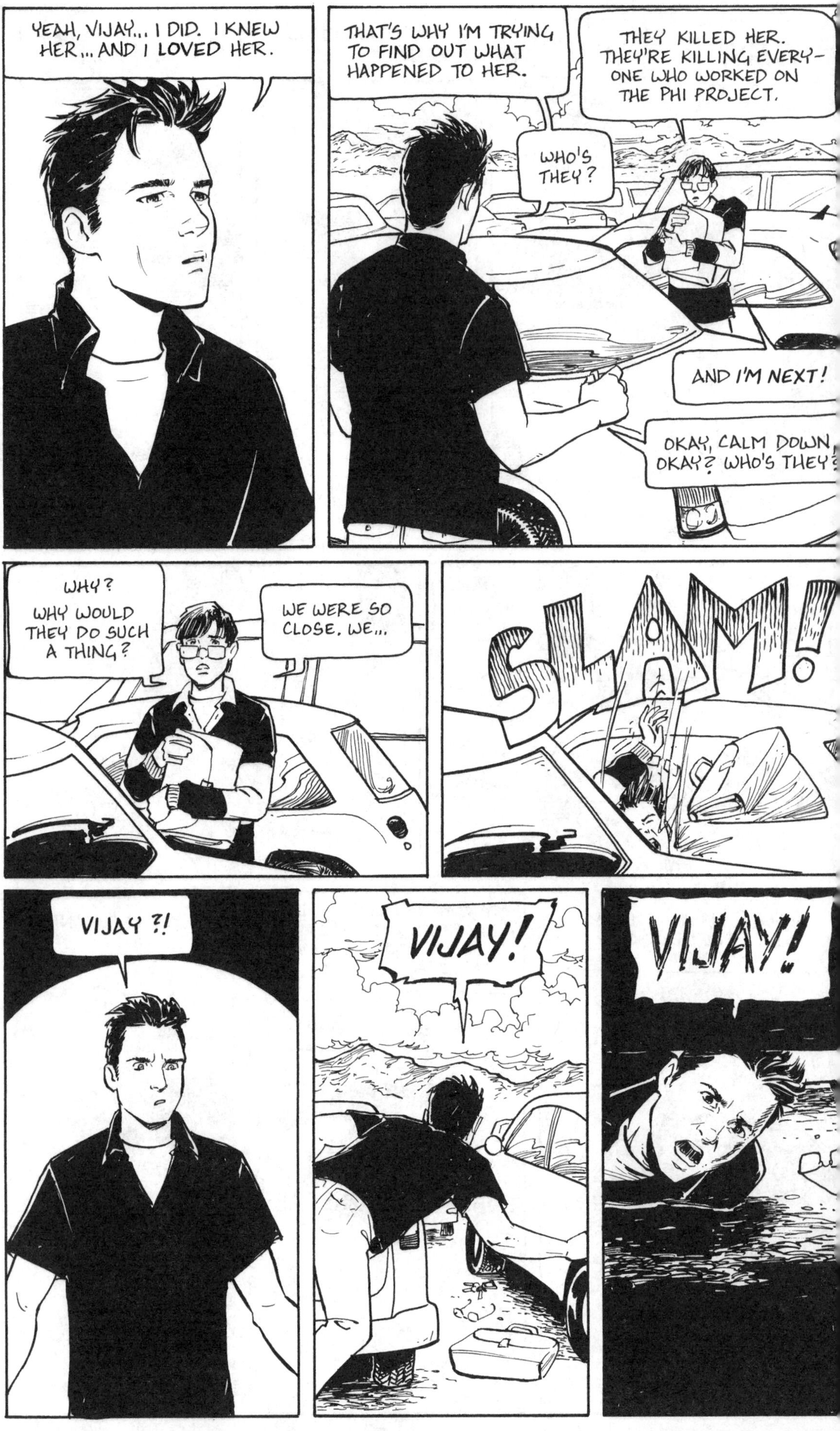
YEAH, VIJAY... I DID. I KNEW HER... AND I LOVED HER.
THAT'S WHY I'M TRYING TO FIND OUT WHAT HAPPENED TO HER.
WHO'S THEY?
THEY KILLED HER. THEY'RE KILLING EVERY-ONE WHO WORKED ON THE PHI PROJECT.
AND I'M NEXT!
OKAY, CALM DOWN, OKAY? WHO'S THEY?
WHY? WHY WOULD THEY DO SUCH A THING?
WE WERE SO CLOSE. WE...
SLAM!
VIJAY ?!
VIJAY!
VIJAY!

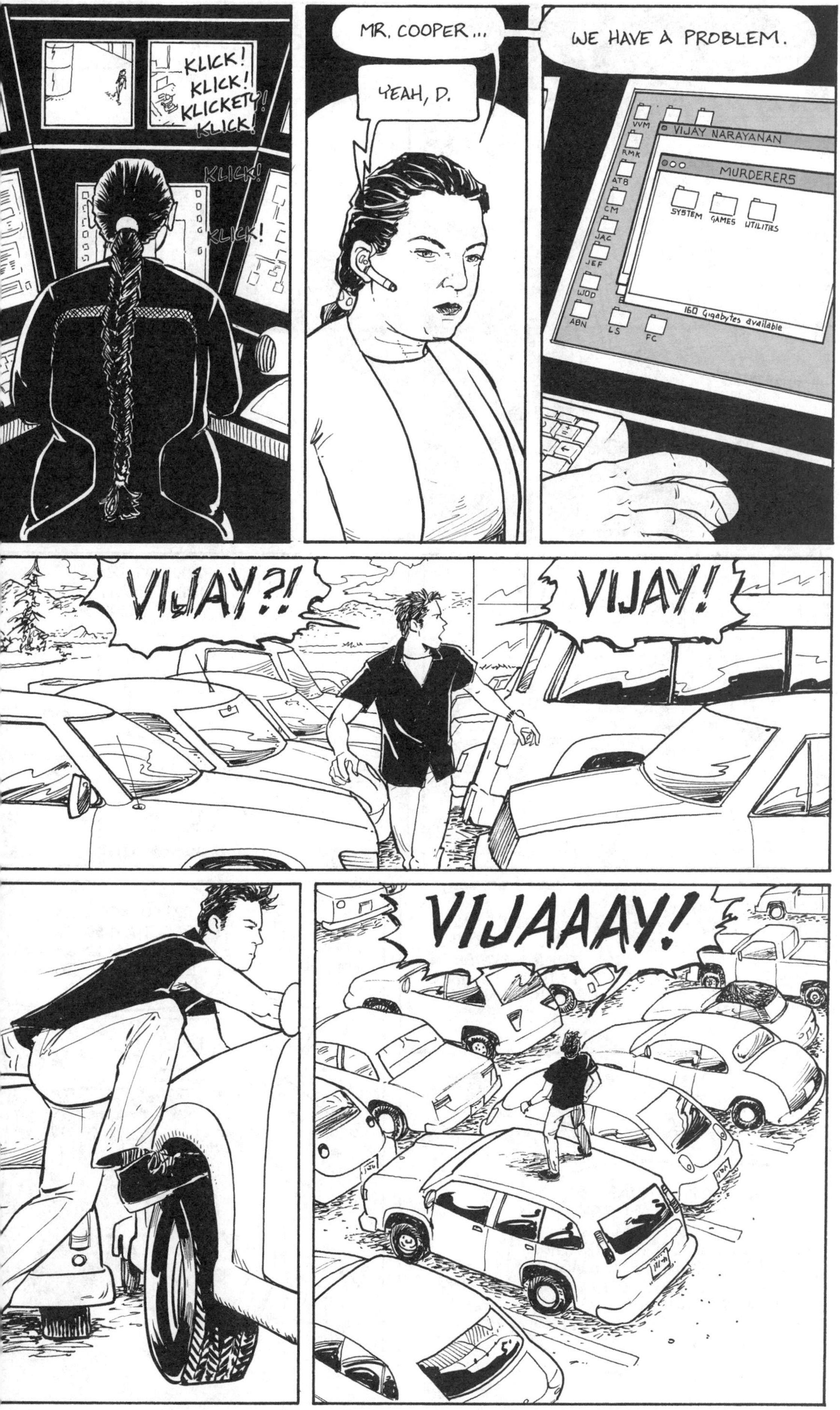
KLICK!
KLICK!
KLICKETY!
KLICK!
KLICK!
KLICK!
MR. COOPER...
YEAH, D.
WE HAVE A PROBLEM.
VIJAY NARAYANAN
MURDERERS
SYSTEM
GAMES
UTILITIES
160 Gigabytes available
VVM
RMK
ATB
CM
JAC
JEF
WOD
ABN
LS
FC
VIJAY?!
VIJAY!
VIJAAAY!

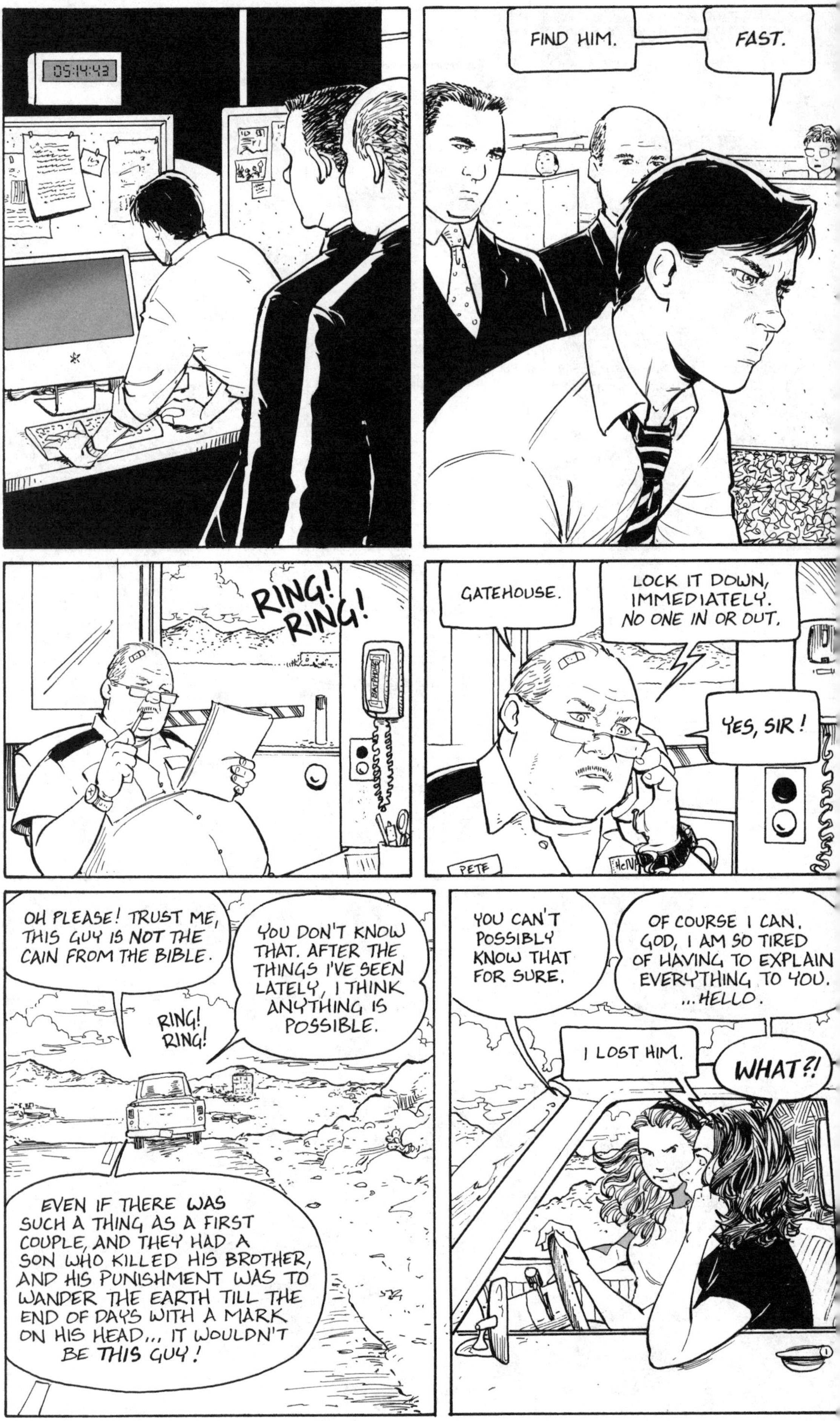
05:14:43
FIND HIM.
FAST.
RING! RING!
GATEHOUSE.
LOCK IT DOWN, IMMEDIATELY. NO ONE IN OR OUT.
YES, SIR!
PETE
OH PLEASE! TRUST ME, THIS GUY IS NOT THE CAIN FROM THE BIBLE.
RING! RING!
YOU DON'T KNOW THAT. AFTER THE THINGS I'VE SEEN LATELY, I THINK ANYTHING IS POSSIBLE.
EVEN IF THERE WAS SUCH A THING AS A FIRST COUPLE, AND THEY HAD A SON WHO KILLED HIS BROTHER, AND HIS PUNISHMENT WAS TO WANDER THE EARTH TILL THE END OF DAYS WITH A MARK ON HIS HEAD,,, IT WOULDN'T BE THIS GUY!
YOU CAN'T POSSIBLY KNOW THAT FOR SURE.
OF COURSE I CAN. GOD, I AM SO TIRED OF HAVING TO EXPLAIN EVERYTHING TO YOU. ...HELLO.
I LOST HIM.
WHAT?!

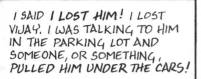

I SAID *I LOST HIM!* I LOST VIJAY. I WAS TALKING TO HIM IN THE PARKING LOT AND SOMEONE, OR SOMETHING, PULLED HIM UNDER THE CARS!

HE'S DISAPPEARED!

DAMMIT, DILLON, I *TOLD* YOU TO WAIT FOR US!

I KNOW. BUT HE WAS LEAVING IN SUCH A HURRY, I WAS AFRAID HE'D GET AWAY.

LOOK, I CAN TELL BY YOUR VOICE YOU'RE UPSET, BUT IF YOU'LL GIVE ME A SEC...

I AM AN EXPERIENCED FIELD AGENT ON A MISSION, YOU IDIOT. I DON'T GET "UPSET"!

YEAH, RIGHT.

MUST BE SOME OTHER REASON WHY YOUR VOICE IS AN OCTAVE HIGHER. IF YOU WILL LET ME FINISH ...

WHAT?

NO WAY.

IVY, LOOK OUT!

KRUNCH!

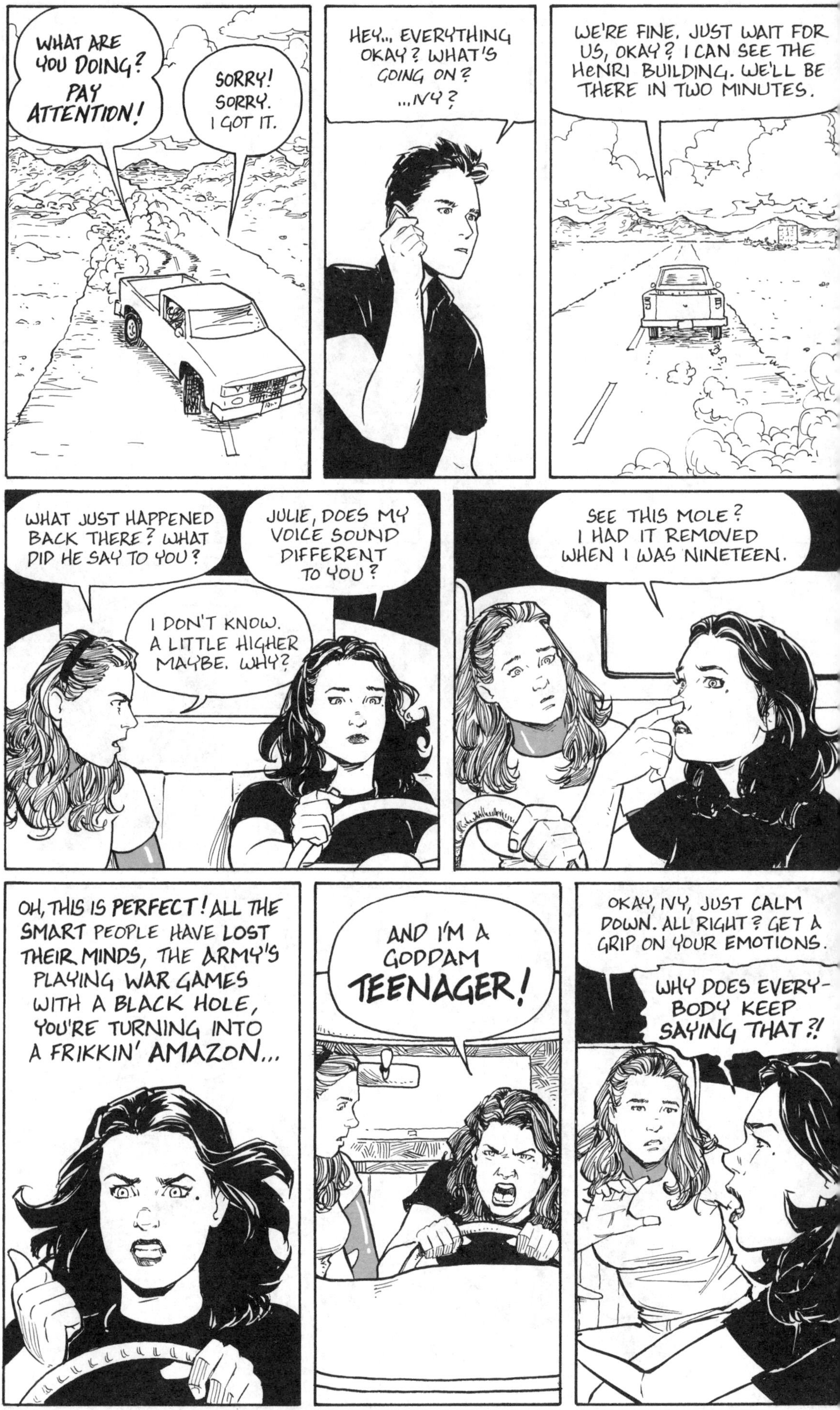
WHAT ARE YOU DOING? PAY ATTENTION!
SORRY! SORRY. I GOT IT.
HEY... EVERYTHING OKAY? WHAT'S GOING ON? ...IVY?
WE'RE FINE. JUST WAIT FOR US, OKAY? I CAN SEE THE HENRI BUILDING. WE'LL BE THERE IN TWO MINUTES.
WHAT JUST HAPPENED BACK THERE? WHAT DID HE SAY TO YOU?
JULIE, DOES MY VOICE SOUND DIFFERENT TO YOU?
I DON'T KNOW. A LITTLE HIGHER MAYBE. WHY?
SEE THIS MOLE? I HAD IT REMOVED WHEN I WAS NINETEEN.
OH, THIS IS PERFECT! ALL THE SMART PEOPLE HAVE LOST THEIR MINDS, THE ARMY'S PLAYING WAR GAMES WITH A BLACK HOLE, YOU'RE TURNING INTO A FRIKKIN' AMAZON...
AND I'M A GODDAM TEENAGER!
OKAY, IVY, JUST CALM DOWN. ALL RIGHT? GET A GRIP ON YOUR EMOTIONS.
WHY DOES EVERY-BODY KEEP SAYING THAT?!

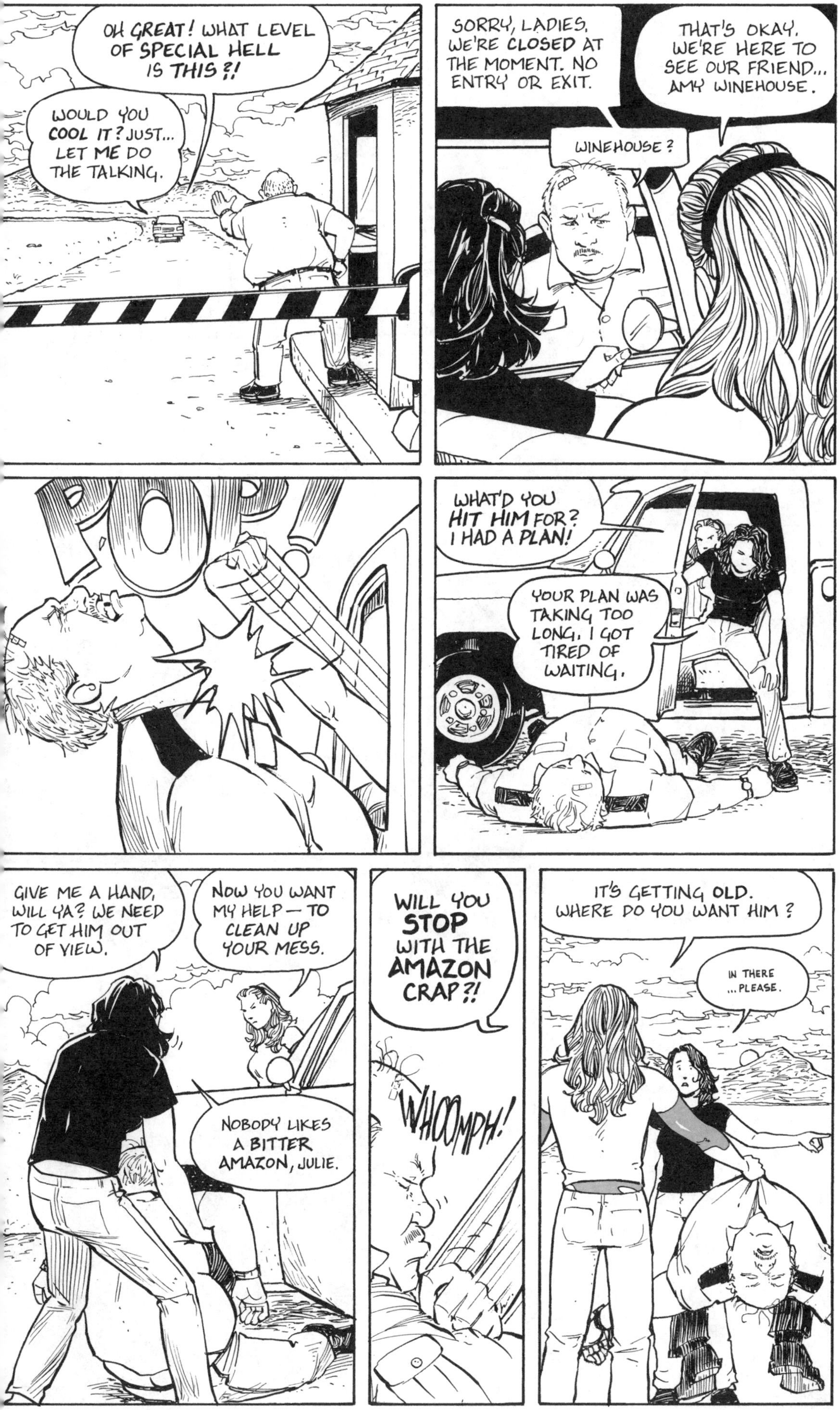
OH GREAT! WHAT LEVEL OF SPECIAL HELL IS THIS?!
WOULD YOU COOL IT? JUST... LET ME DO THE TALKING.
SORRY, LADIES. WE'RE CLOSED AT THE MOMENT. NO ENTRY OR EXIT.
THAT'S OKAY. WE'RE HERE TO SEE OUR FRIEND... AMY WINEHOUSE.
WINEHOUSE?
WHAT'D YOU HIT HIM FOR? I HAD A PLAN!
YOUR PLAN WAS TAKING TOO LONG. I GOT TIRED OF WAITING.
GIVE ME A HAND, WILL YA? WE NEED TO GET HIM OUT OF VIEW.
NOW YOU WANT MY HELP — TO CLEAN UP YOUR MESS.
NOBODY LIKES A BITTER AMAZON, JULIE.
WILL YOU STOP WITH THE AMAZON CRAP?!
WHOOMPH!
IT'S GETTING OLD. WHERE DO YOU WANT HIM?
IN THERE ...PLEASE.

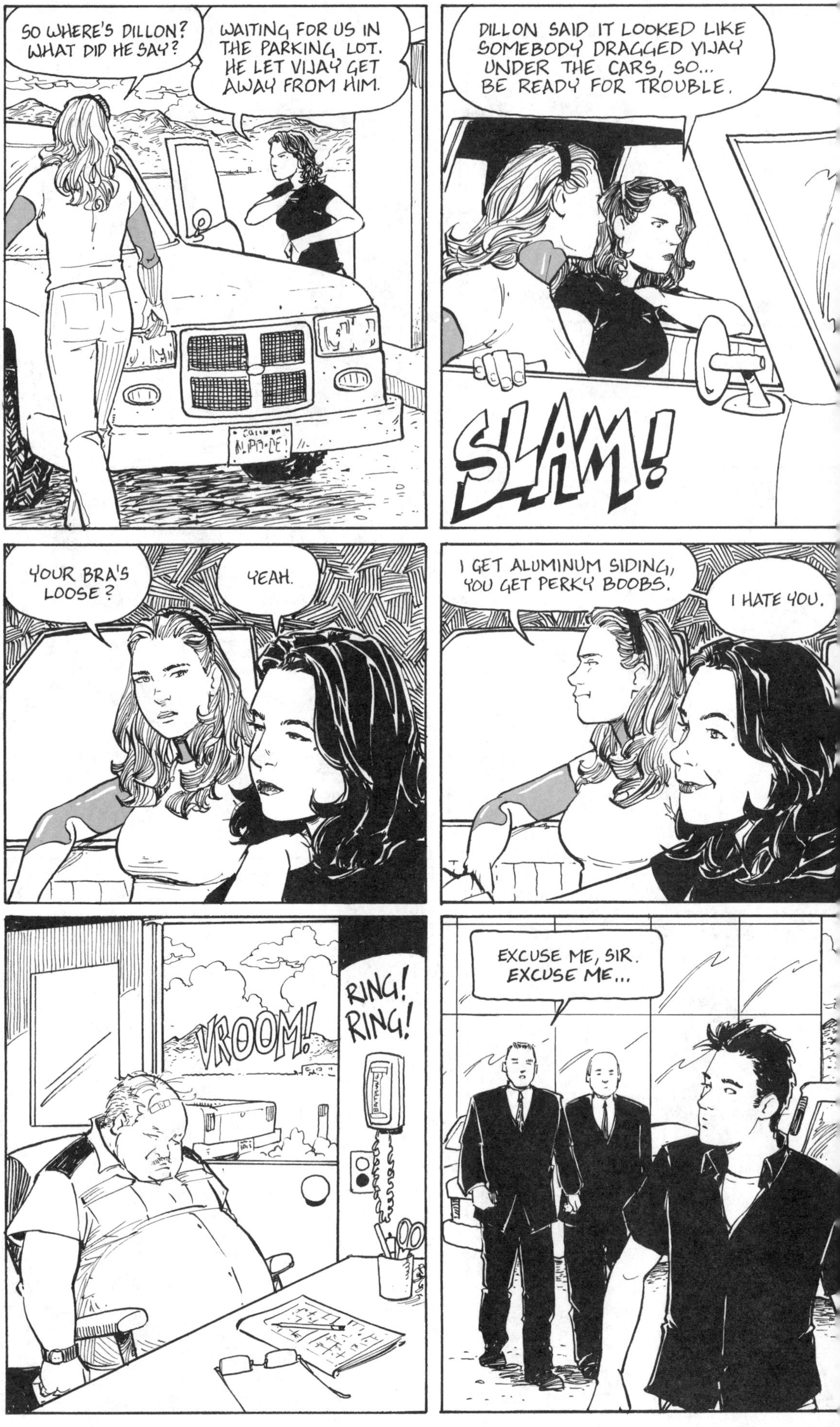
SO WHERE'S DILLON? WHAT DID HE SAY?
WAITING FOR US IN THE PARKING LOT. HE LET VIJAY GET AWAY FROM HIM.
DILLON SAID IT LOOKED LIKE SOMEBODY DRAGGED VIJAY UNDER THE CARS, SO... BE READY FOR TROUBLE.
SLAM!
YOUR BRA'S LOOSE?
YEAH.
I GET ALUMINUM SIDING, YOU GET PERKY BOOBS.
I HATE YOU.
VROOM!
RING! RING!
EXCUSE ME, SIR. EXCUSE ME...

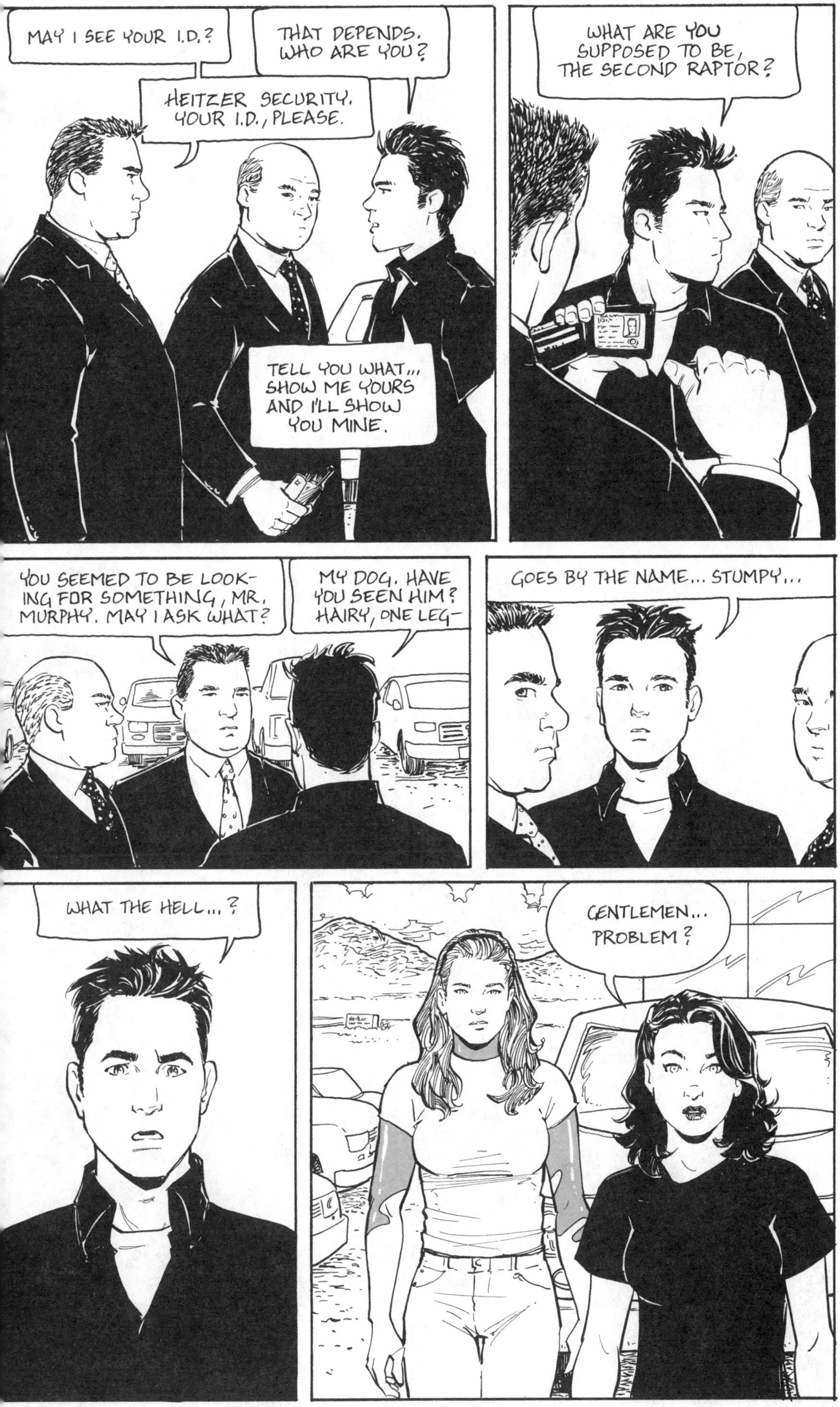

MAY I SEE YOUR I.D.?
THAT DEPENDS. WHO ARE YOU?
HEITZER SECURITY. YOUR I.D., PLEASE.
TELL YOU WHAT... SHOW ME YOURS AND I'LL SHOW YOU MINE.
WHAT ARE YOU SUPPOSED TO BE, THE SECOND RAPTOR?
YOU SEEMED TO BE LOOKING FOR SOMETHING, MR. MURPHY. MAY I ASK WHAT?
MY DOG. HAVE YOU SEEN HIM? HAIRY, ONE LEG-
GOES BY THE NAME... STUMPY...
WHAT THE HELL...?
GENTLEMEN... PROBLEM?

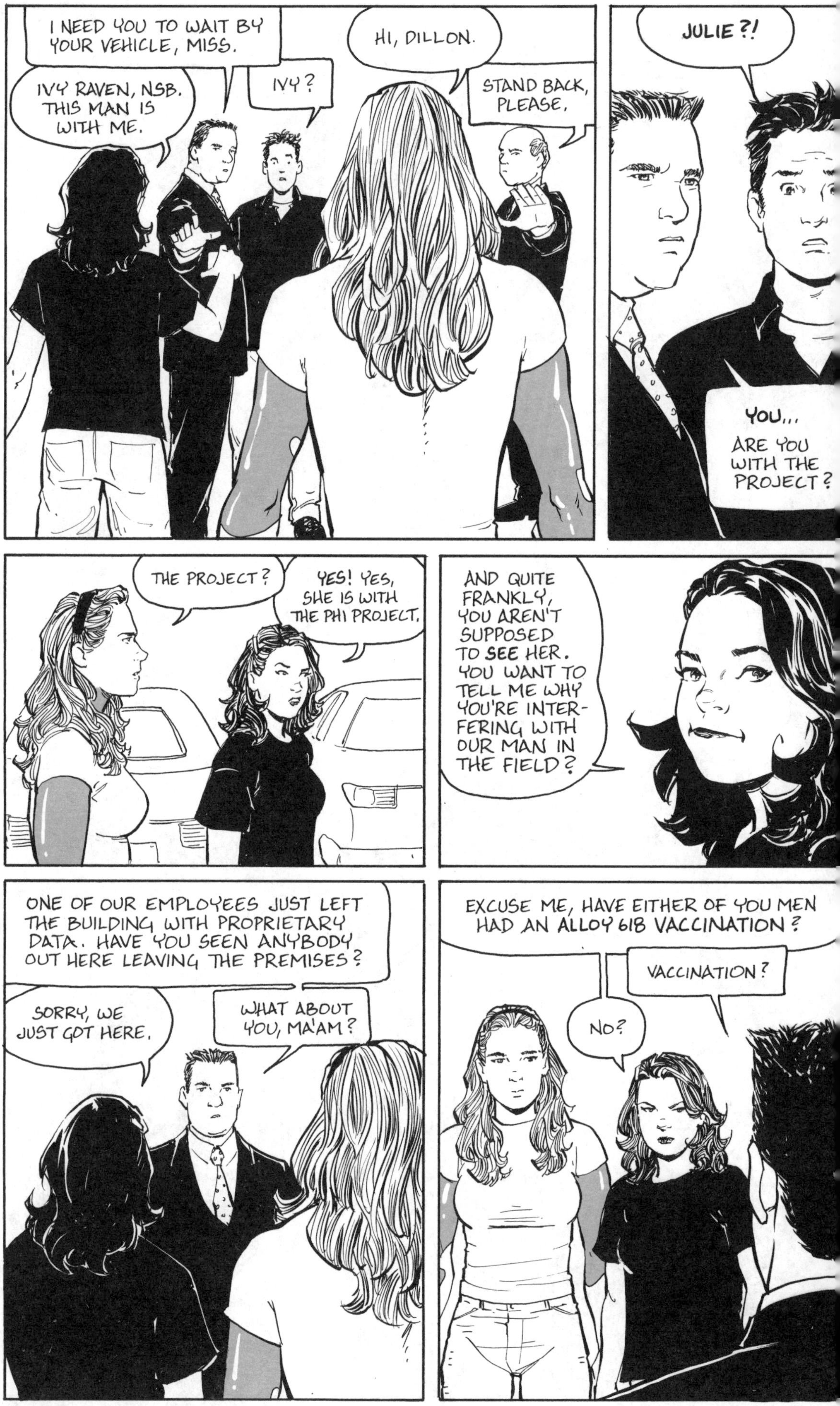
I NEED YOU TO WAIT BY YOUR VEHICLE, MISS.
IVY RAVEN, NSB. THIS MAN IS WITH ME.
IVY?
HI, DILLON.
STAND BACK, PLEASE.
JULIE?!
YOU... ARE YOU WITH THE PROJECT?
THE PROJECT?
YES! YES, SHE IS WITH THE PHI PROJECT.
AND QUITE FRANKLY, YOU AREN'T SUPPOSED TO SEE HER. YOU WANT TO TELL ME WHY YOU'RE INTERFERING WITH OUR MAN IN THE FIELD?
ONE OF OUR EMPLOYEES JUST LEFT THE BUILDING WITH PROPRIETARY DATA. HAVE YOU SEEN ANYBODY OUT HERE LEAVING THE PREMISES?
SORRY, WE JUST GOT HERE.
WHAT ABOUT YOU, MA'AM?
EXCUSE ME, HAVE EITHER OF YOU MEN HAD AN ALLOY 618 VACCINATION?
VACCINATION?
NO?

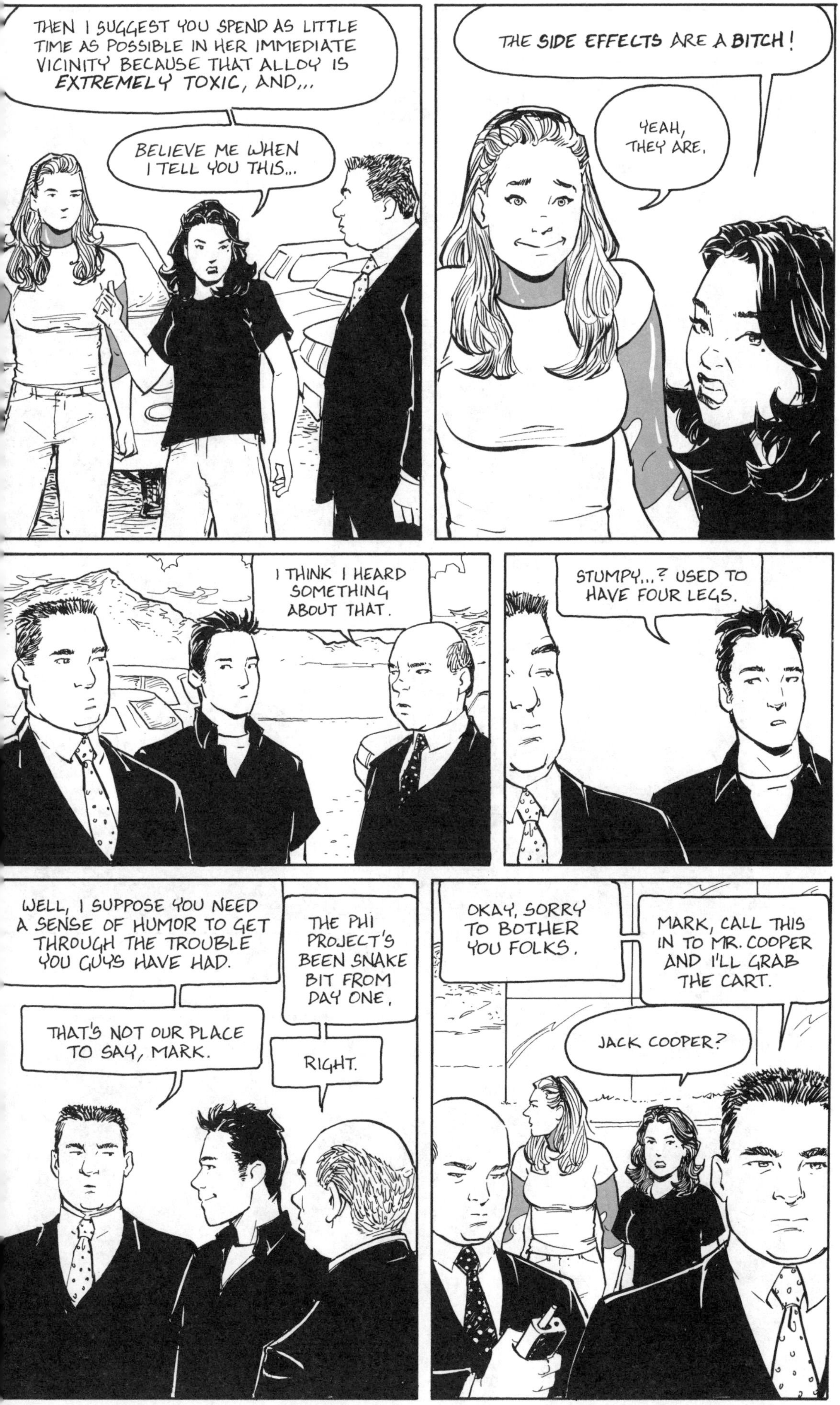
THEN I SUGGEST YOU SPEND AS LITTLE TIME AS POSSIBLE IN HER IMMEDIATE VICINITY BECAUSE THAT ALLOY IS EXTREMELY TOXIC, AND...
BELIEVE ME WHEN I TELL YOU THIS...
THE SIDE EFFECTS ARE A BITCH!
YEAH, THEY ARE.
I THINK I HEARD SOMETHING ABOUT THAT.
STUMPY...? USED TO HAVE FOUR LEGS.
WELL, I SUPPOSE YOU NEED A SENSE OF HUMOR TO GET THROUGH THE TROUBLE YOU GUYS HAVE HAD.
THAT'S NOT OUR PLACE TO SAY, MARK.
THE PHI PROJECT'S BEEN SNAKE BIT FROM DAY ONE.
RIGHT.
OKAY, SORRY TO BOTHER YOU FOLKS.
MARK, CALL THIS IN TO MR. COOPER AND I'LL GRAB THE CART.
JACK COOPER?

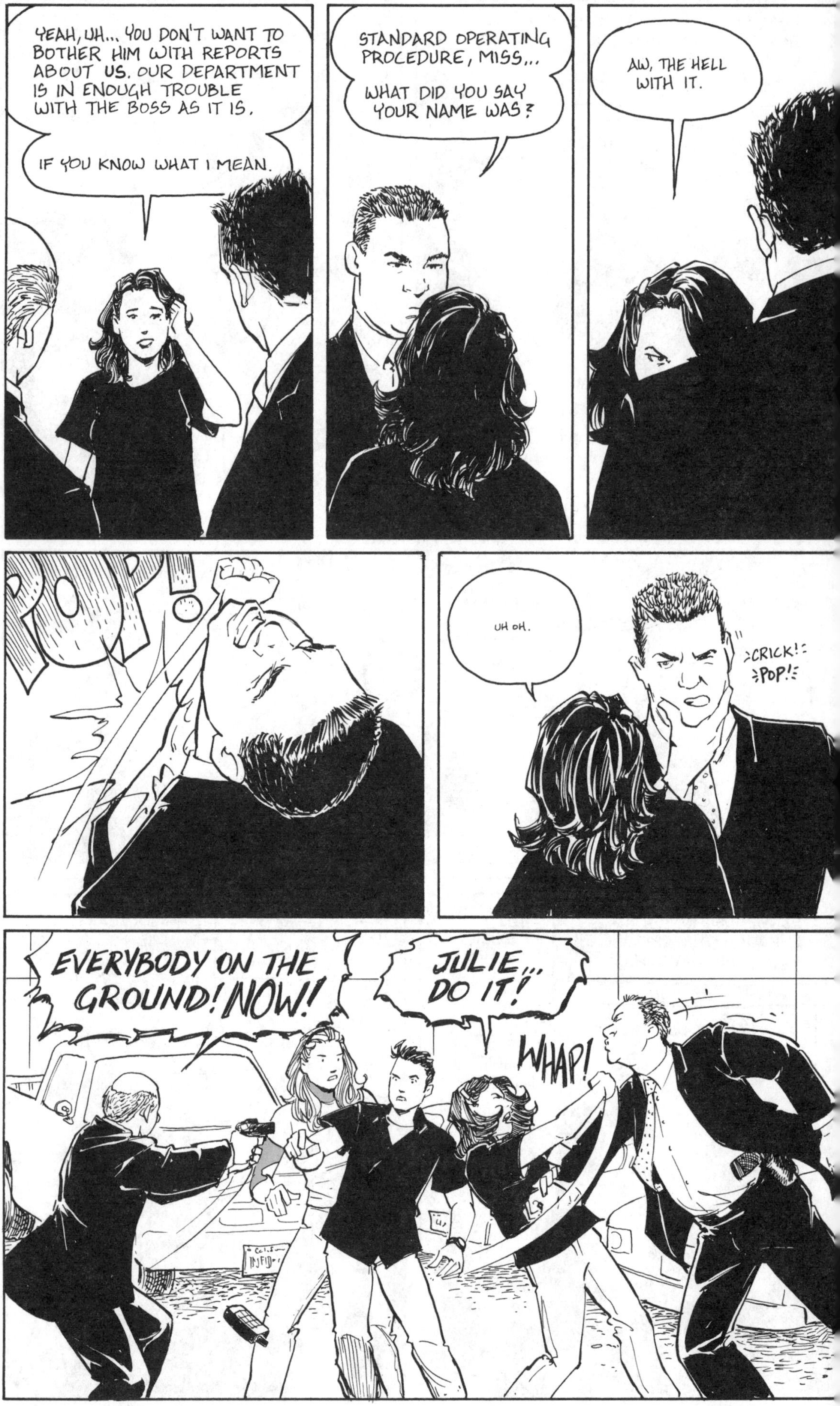
YEAH, UH... YOU DON'T WANT TO BOTHER HIM WITH REPORTS ABOUT US. OUR DEPARTMENT IS IN ENOUGH TROUBLE WITH THE BOSS AS IT IS.
IF YOU KNOW WHAT I MEAN.
STANDARD OPERATING PROCEDURE, MISS...
WHAT DID YOU SAY YOUR NAME WAS?
AW, THE HELL WITH IT.
POP!
UH OH.
CRICK!
POP!
EVERYBODY ON THE GROUND! NOW!
JULIE... DO IT!
WHAP!

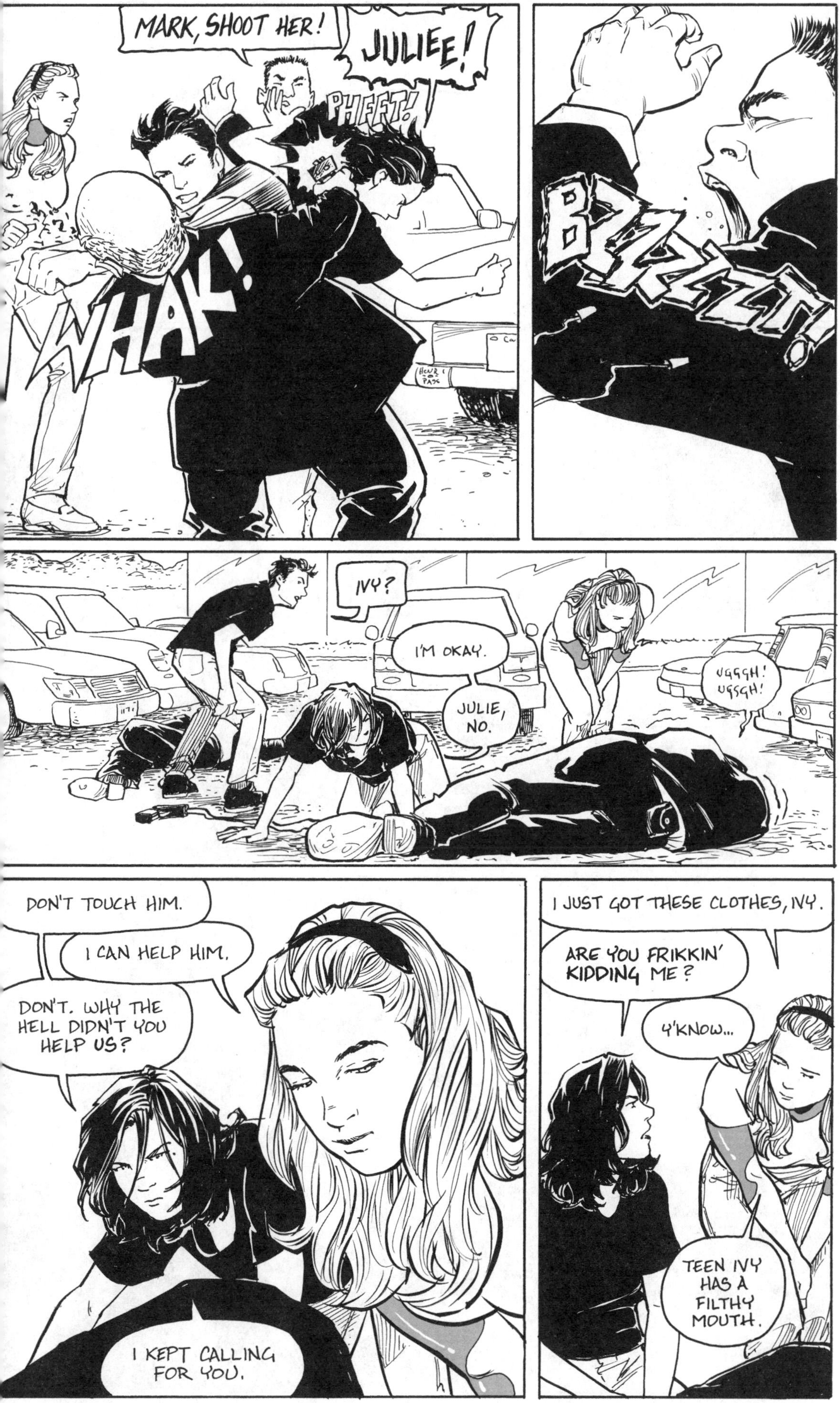
MARK, SHOOT HER!
JULIEE!
PHFFT!
WHAK!
BZZZT!
IVY?
I'M OKAY.
JULIE, NO.
UGGGH! UGGGH!
DON'T TOUCH HIM.
I CAN HELP HIM.
DON'T. WHY THE HELL DIDN'T YOU HELP US?
I KEPT CALLING FOR YOU.
I JUST GOT THESE CLOTHES, IVY.
ARE YOU FRIKKIN' KIDDING ME?
Y'KNOW...
TEEN IVY HAS A FILTHY MOUTH.

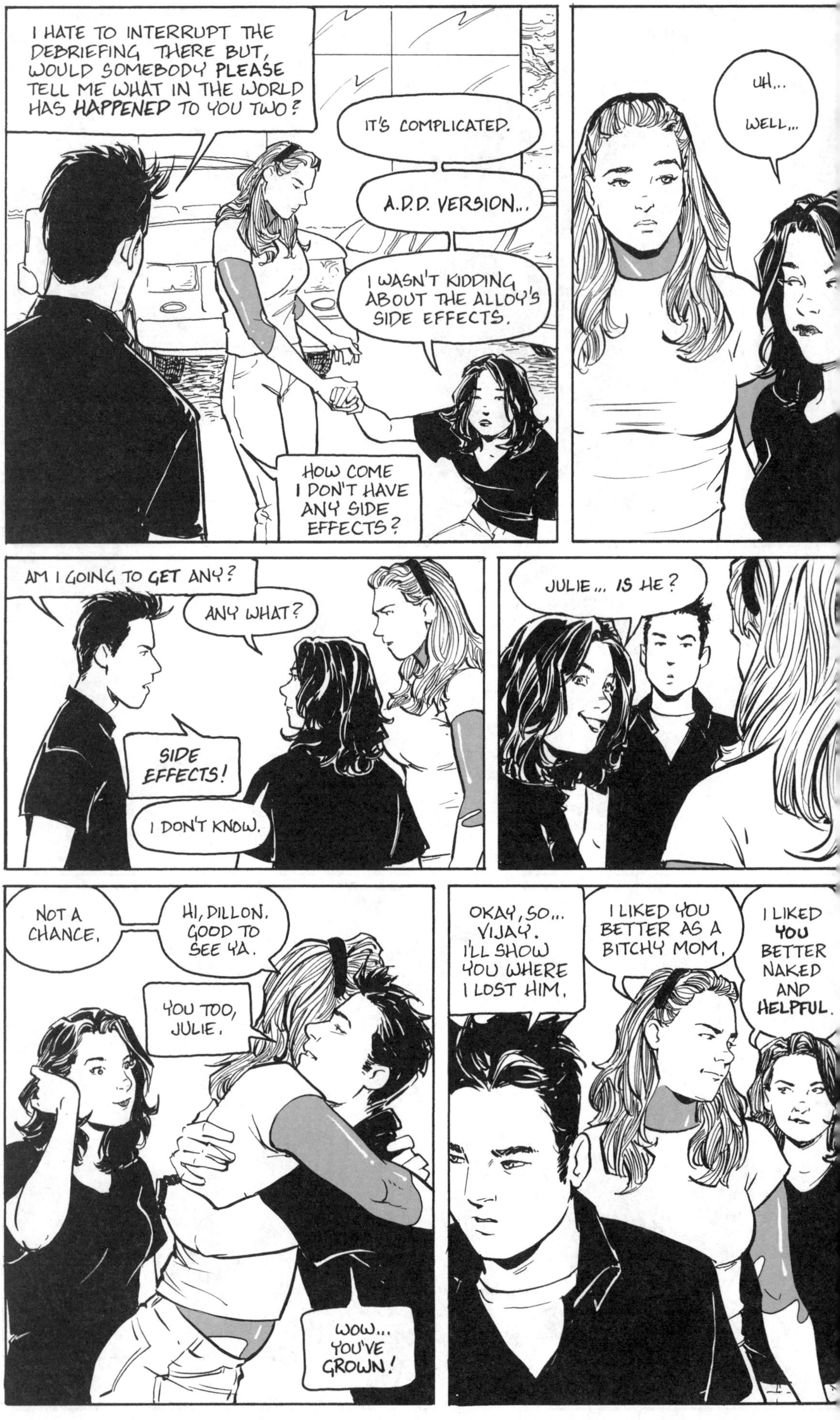
I HATE TO INTERRUPT THE DEBRIEFING THERE BUT, WOULD SOMEBODY **PLEASE** TELL ME WHAT IN THE WORLD HAS **HAPPENED** TO YOU TWO?
IT'S COMPLICATED.
A.D.D. VERSION...
I WASN'T KIDDING ABOUT THE ALLOY'S SIDE EFFECTS.
HOW COME I DON'T HAVE ANY SIDE EFFECTS?
UH...
WELL...
AM I GOING TO **GET** ANY?
ANY WHAT?
SIDE EFFECTS!
I DON'T KNOW.
JULIE... **IS** HE?
NOT A CHANCE.
HI, DILLON. GOOD TO SEE YA.
YOU TOO, JULIE.
WOW... YOU'VE GROWN!
OKAY, SO... VIJAY. I'LL SHOW YOU WHERE I LOST HIM.
I LIKED YOU BETTER AS A BITCHY MOM.
I LIKED **YOU** BETTER NAKED AND **HELPFUL**.

I WAS STANDING OVER THERE...

AND VIJAY WAS HERE, BETWEEN THE CARS, WHEN HE DROPPED OUT OF SIGHT.

I LOOKED UNDER ALL THESE CARS, BUT... NO SIGN OF HIM ANYWHERE. HE JUST VANISHED.

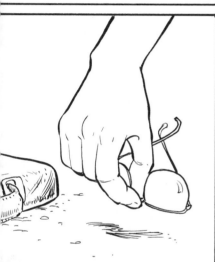

DO YOU GUYS FEEL THAT?

FEEL WHAT?

FEAR.

"The priest is to sprinkle the blood against the altar
of the Lord at the entrance to the Tent of Meeting
and burn the fat as an aroma pleasing to the Lord.
— Leviticus 17:6

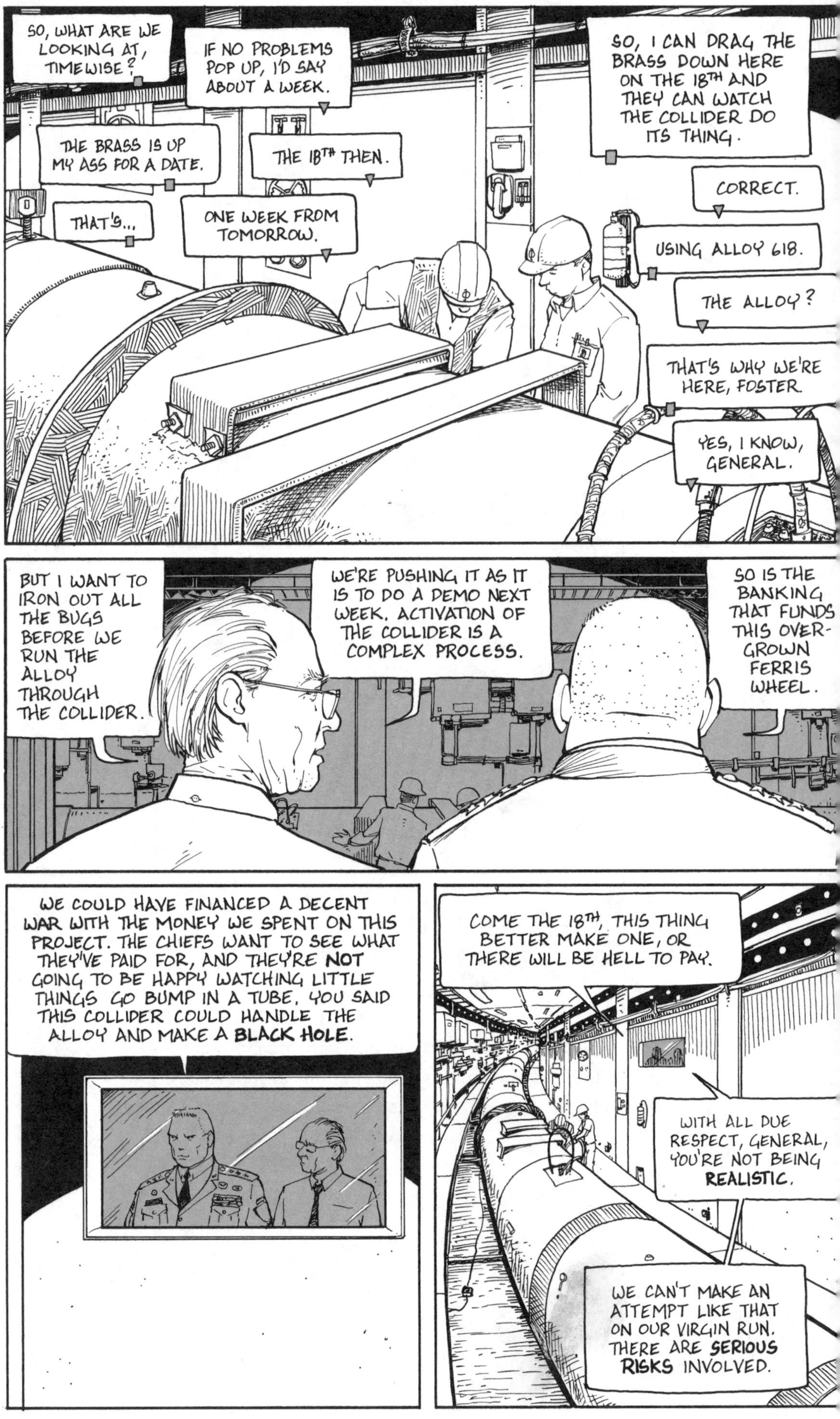
SO, WHAT ARE WE LOOKING AT, TIMEWISE?
IF NO PROBLEMS POP UP, I'D SAY ABOUT A WEEK.
THE BRASS IS UP MY ASS FOR A DATE.
THE 18TH THEN.
THAT'S...
ONE WEEK FROM TOMORROW.
SO, I CAN DRAG THE BRASS DOWN HERE ON THE 18TH AND THEY CAN WATCH THE COLLIDER DO ITS THING.
CORRECT.
USING ALLOY 618.
THE ALLOY?
THAT'S WHY WE'RE HERE, FOSTER.
YES, I KNOW, GENERAL.
BUT I WANT TO IRON OUT ALL THE BUGS BEFORE WE RUN THE ALLOY THROUGH THE COLLIDER.
WE'RE PUSHING IT AS IT IS TO DO A DEMO NEXT WEEK. ACTIVATION OF THE COLLIDER IS A COMPLEX PROCESS.
SO IS THE BANKING THAT FUNDS THIS OVER-GROWN FERRIS WHEEL.
WE COULD HAVE FINANCED A DECENT WAR WITH THE MONEY WE SPENT ON THIS PROJECT. THE CHIEFS WANT TO SEE WHAT THEY'VE PAID FOR, AND THEY'RE **NOT** GOING TO BE HAPPY WATCHING LITTLE THINGS GO BUMP IN A TUBE. YOU SAID THIS COLLIDER COULD HANDLE THE ALLOY AND MAKE A **BLACK HOLE**.
COME THE 18TH, THIS THING BETTER MAKE ONE, OR THERE WILL BE HELL TO PAY.
WITH ALL DUE RESPECT, GENERAL, YOU'RE NOT BEING **REALISTIC**.
WE CAN'T MAKE AN ATTEMPT LIKE THAT ON OUR VIRGIN RUN. THERE ARE **SERIOUS RISKS** INVOLVED.

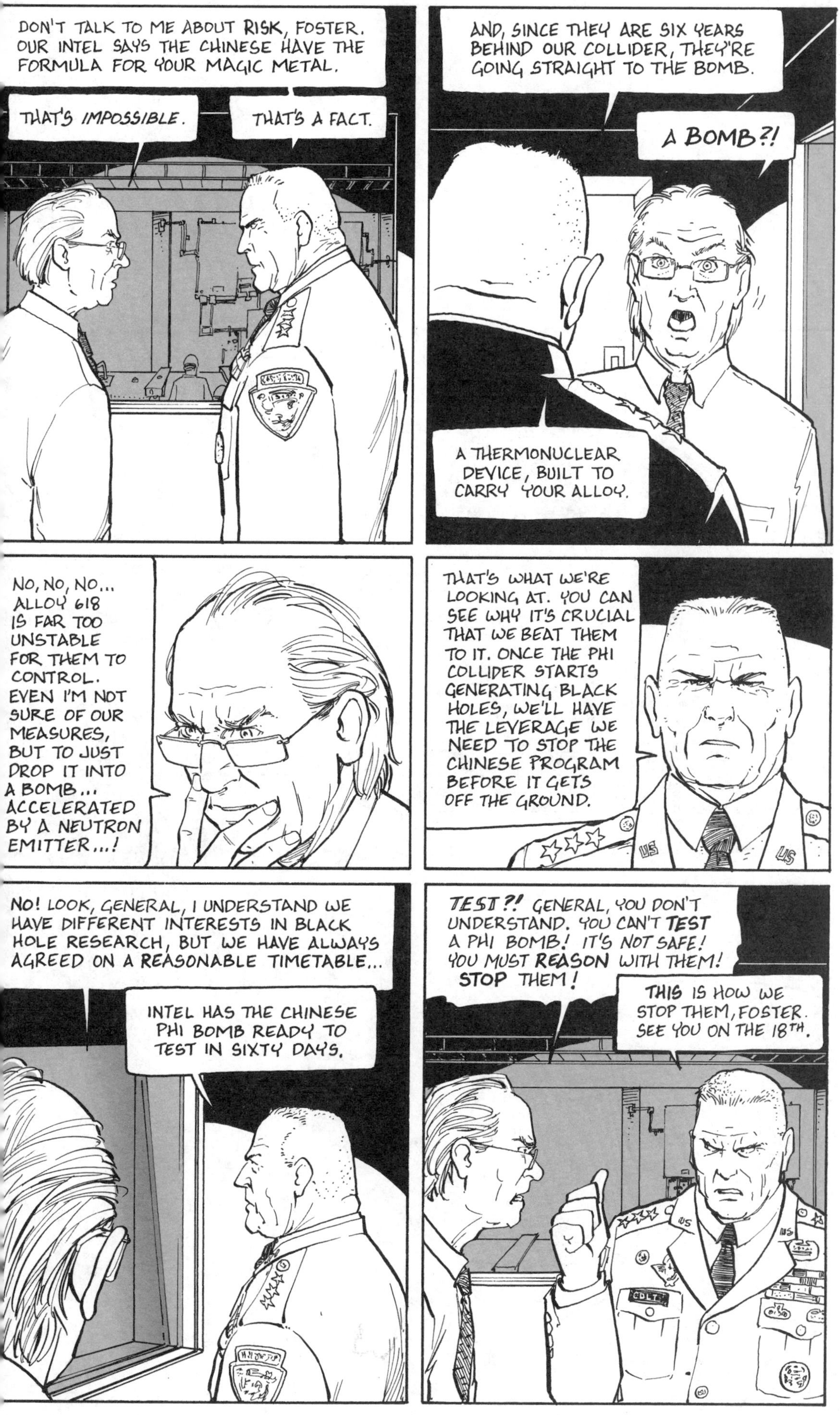
DON'T TALK TO ME ABOUT RISK, FOSTER. OUR INTEL SAYS THE CHINESE HAVE THE FORMULA FOR YOUR MAGIC METAL.
THAT'S IMPOSSIBLE.
THAT'S A FACT.
AND, SINCE THEY ARE SIX YEARS BEHIND OUR COLLIDER, THEY'RE GOING STRAIGHT TO THE BOMB.
A BOMB?!
A THERMONUCLEAR DEVICE, BUILT TO CARRY YOUR ALLOY.
NO, NO, NO... ALLOY 618 IS FAR TOO UNSTABLE FOR THEM TO CONTROL. EVEN I'M NOT SURE OF OUR MEASURES, BUT TO JUST DROP IT INTO A BOMB... ACCELERATED BY A NEUTRON EMITTER...!
THAT'S WHAT WE'RE LOOKING AT. YOU CAN SEE WHY IT'S CRUCIAL THAT WE BEAT THEM TO IT. ONCE THE PHI COLLIDER STARTS GENERATING BLACK HOLES, WE'LL HAVE THE LEVERAGE WE NEED TO STOP THE CHINESE PROGRAM BEFORE IT GETS OFF THE GROUND.
NO! LOOK, GENERAL, I UNDERSTAND WE HAVE DIFFERENT INTERESTS IN BLACK HOLE RESEARCH, BUT WE HAVE ALWAYS AGREED ON A REASONABLE TIMETABLE...
INTEL HAS THE CHINESE PHI BOMB READY TO TEST IN SIXTY DAYS.
TEST?! GENERAL, YOU DON'T UNDERSTAND. YOU CAN'T TEST A PHI BOMB! IT'S NOT SAFE! YOU MUST REASON WITH THEM! STOP THEM!
THIS IS HOW WE STOP THEM, FOSTER. SEE YOU ON THE 18TH.

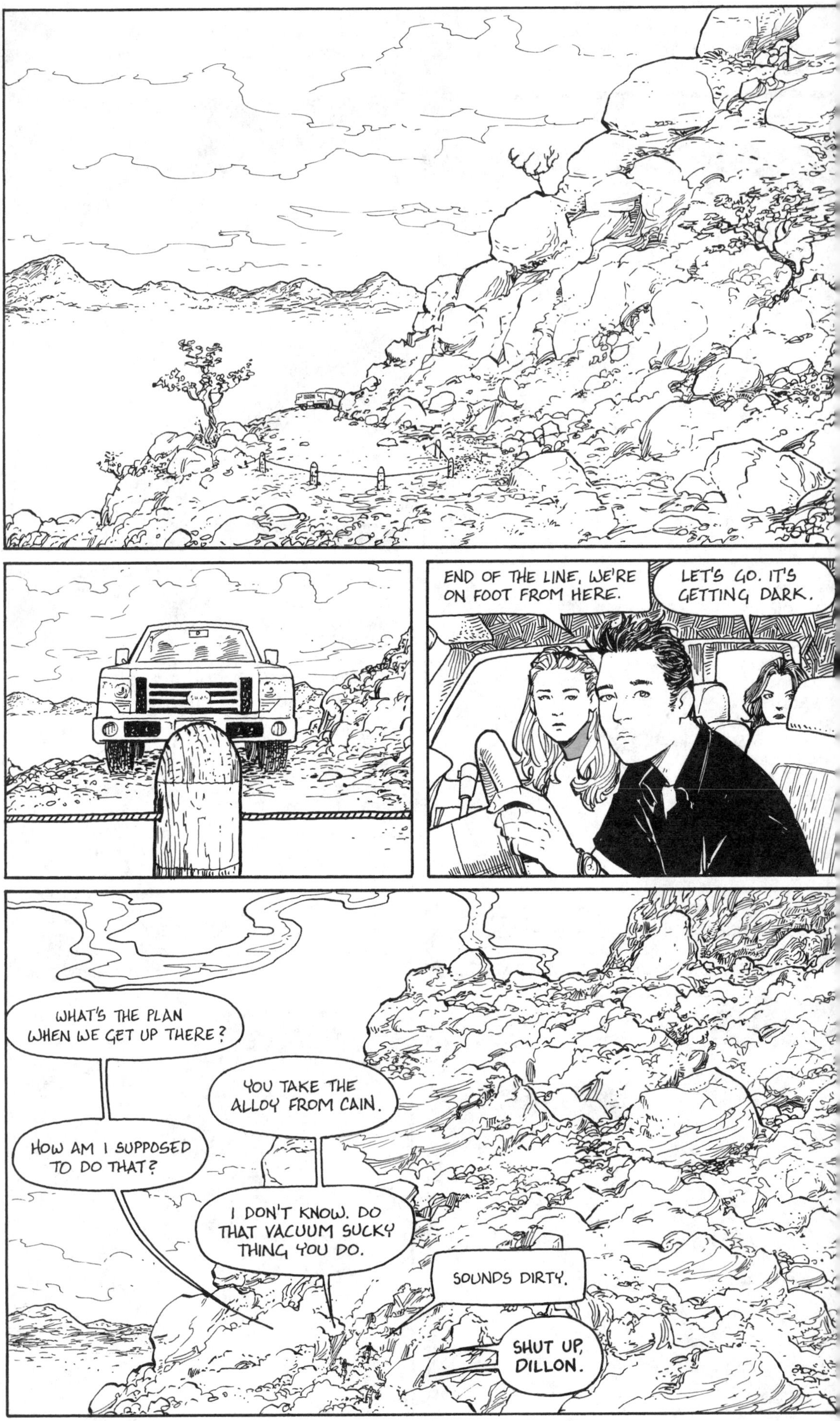
END OF THE LINE, WE'RE ON FOOT FROM HERE.
LET'S GO. IT'S GETTING DARK.
WHAT'S THE PLAN WHEN WE GET UP THERE?
YOU TAKE THE ALLOY FROM CAIN.
HOW AM I SUPPOSED TO DO THAT?
I DON'T KNOW. DO THAT VACUUM SUCKY THING YOU DO.
SOUNDS DIRTY.
SHUT UP, DILLON.

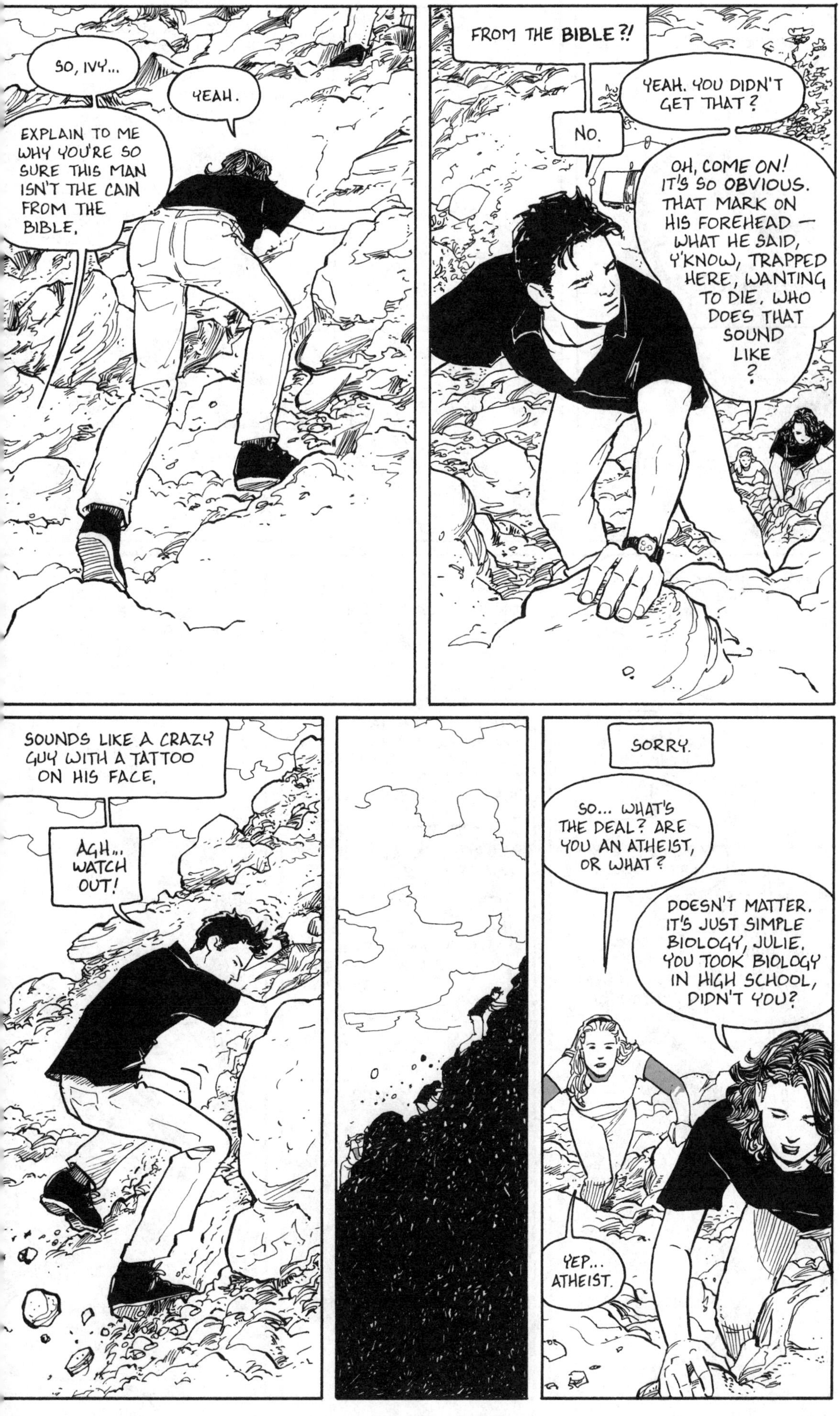
SO, IVY...
YEAH.
EXPLAIN TO ME WHY YOU'RE SO SURE THIS MAN ISN'T THE CAIN FROM THE BIBLE.
FROM THE BIBLE?!
NO.
YEAH. YOU DIDN'T GET THAT?
OH, COME ON! IT'S SO OBVIOUS. THAT MARK ON HIS FOREHEAD — WHAT HE SAID, Y'KNOW, TRAPPED HERE, WANTING TO DIE. WHO DOES THAT SOUND LIKE?
SOUNDS LIKE A CRAZY GUY WITH A TATTOO ON HIS FACE.
AGH... WATCH OUT!
SORRY.
SO... WHAT'S THE DEAL? ARE YOU AN ATHEIST, OR WHAT?
DOESN'T MATTER. IT'S JUST SIMPLE BIOLOGY, JULIE. YOU TOOK BIOLOGY IN HIGH SCHOOL, DIDN'T YOU?
YEP... ATHEIST.

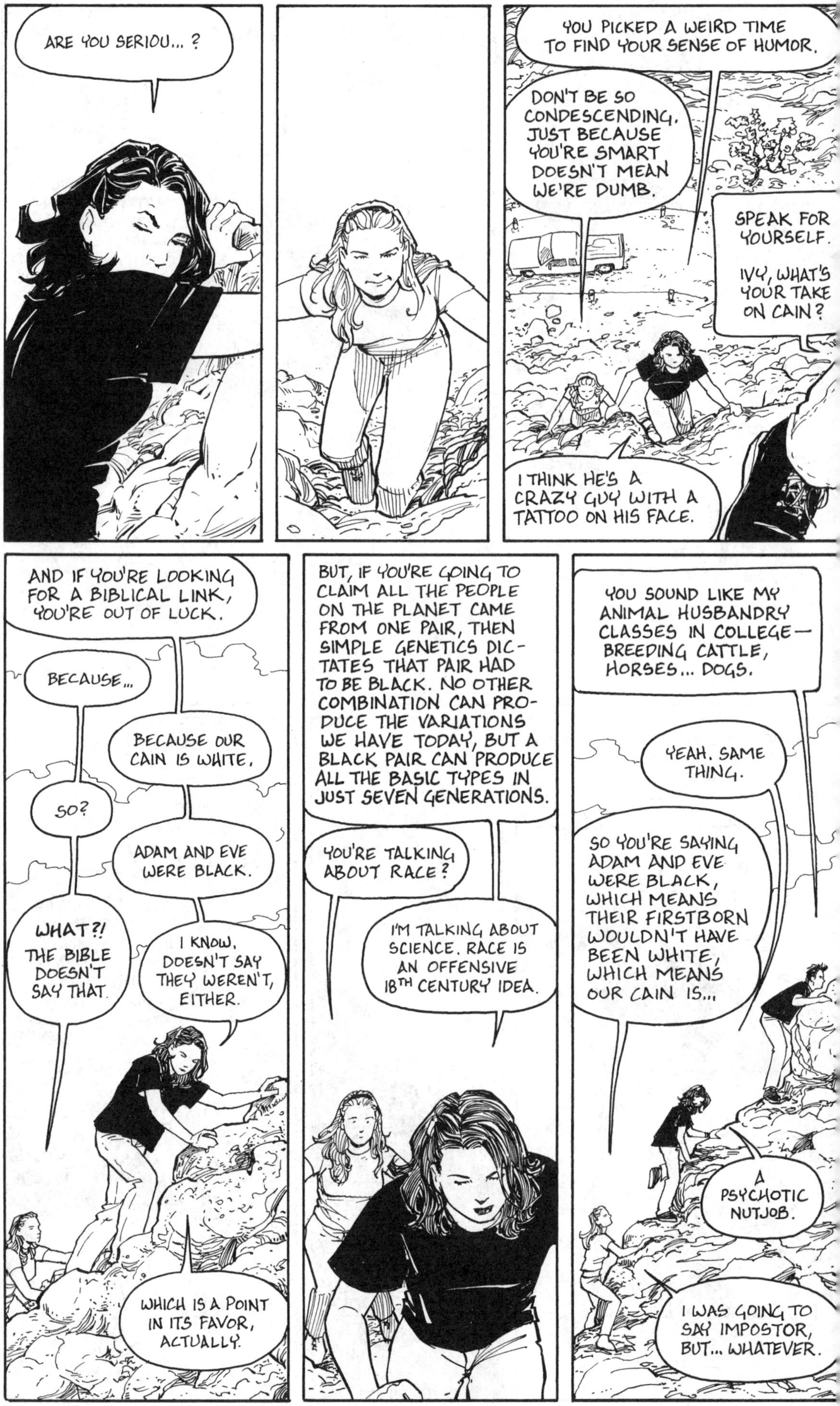
ARE YOU SERIOU... ?
YOU PICKED A WEIRD TIME TO FIND YOUR SENSE OF HUMOR.
DON'T BE SO CONDESCENDING. JUST BECAUSE YOU'RE SMART DOESN'T MEAN WE'RE DUMB.
SPEAK FOR YOURSELF.
IVY, WHAT'S YOUR TAKE ON CAIN?
I THINK HE'S A CRAZY GUY WITH A TATTOO ON HIS FACE.
AND IF YOU'RE LOOKING FOR A BIBLICAL LINK, YOU'RE OUT OF LUCK.
BECAUSE...
BECAUSE OUR CAIN IS WHITE.
SO?
ADAM AND EVE WERE BLACK.
WHAT?! THE BIBLE DOESN'T SAY THAT.
I KNOW. DOESN'T SAY THEY WEREN'T, EITHER.
WHICH IS A POINT IN ITS FAVOR, ACTUALLY.
BUT, IF YOU'RE GOING TO CLAIM ALL THE PEOPLE ON THE PLANET CAME FROM ONE PAIR, THEN SIMPLE GENETICS DICTATES THAT PAIR HAD TO BE BLACK. NO OTHER COMBINATION CAN PRODUCE THE VARIATIONS WE HAVE TODAY, BUT A BLACK PAIR CAN PRODUCE ALL THE BASIC TYPES IN JUST SEVEN GENERATIONS.
YOU'RE TALKING ABOUT RACE?
I'M TALKING ABOUT SCIENCE. RACE IS AN OFFENSIVE 18TH CENTURY IDEA.
YOU SOUND LIKE MY ANIMAL HUSBANDRY CLASSES IN COLLEGE— BREEDING CATTLE, HORSES... DOGS.
YEAH. SAME THING.
SO YOU'RE SAYING ADAM AND EVE WERE BLACK, WHICH MEANS THEIR FIRSTBORN WOULDN'T HAVE BEEN WHITE, WHICH MEANS OUR CAIN IS...
A PSYCHOTIC NUTJOB.
I WAS GOING TO SAY IMPOSTOR, BUT... WHATEVER.

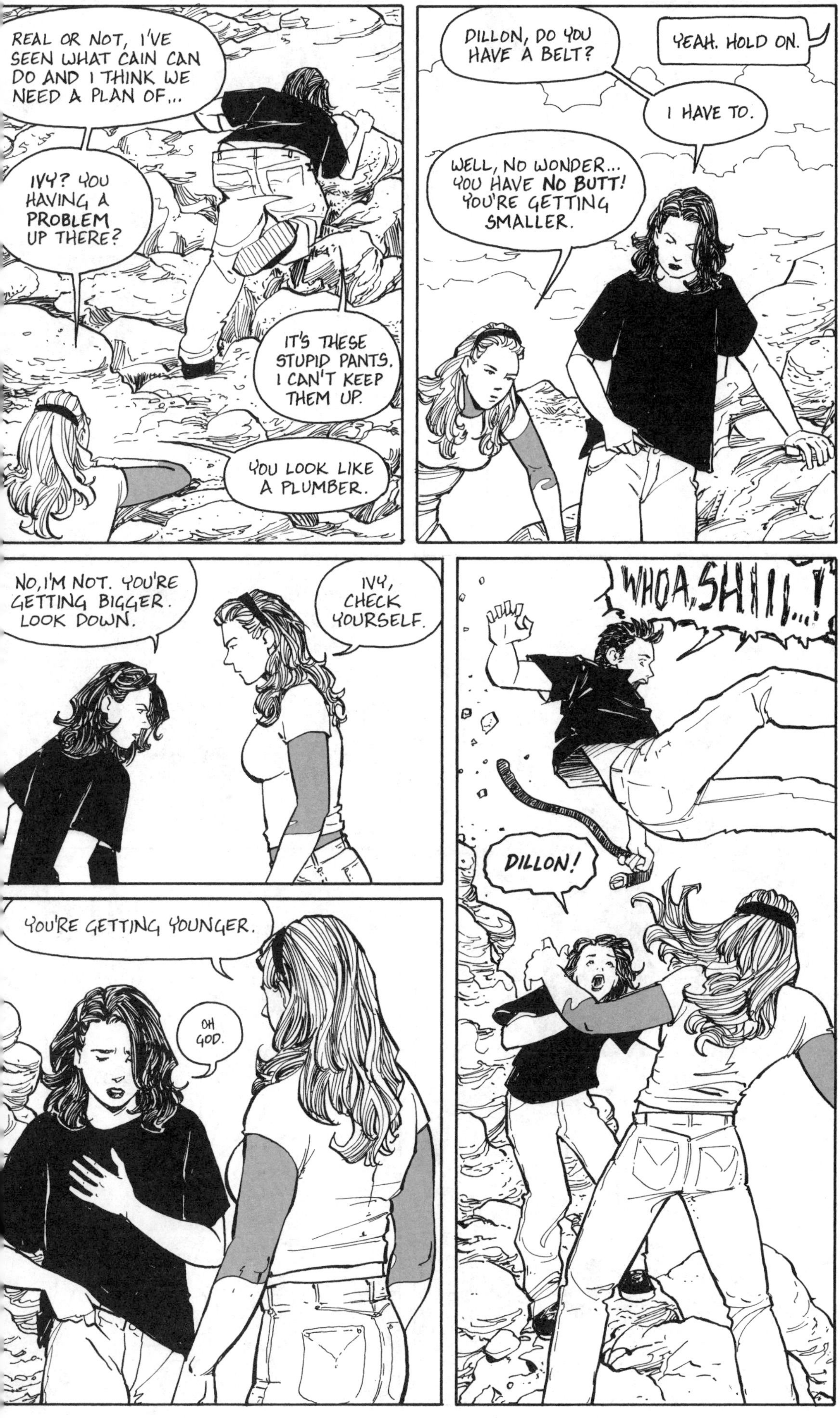
REAL OR NOT, I'VE SEEN WHAT CAIN CAN DO AND I THINK WE NEED A PLAN OF...
IVY? YOU HAVING A PROBLEM UP THERE?
IT'S THESE STUPID PANTS. I CAN'T KEEP THEM UP.
YOU LOOK LIKE A PLUMBER.
DILLON, DO YOU HAVE A BELT?
YEAH. HOLD ON.
I HAVE TO.
WELL, NO WONDER... YOU HAVE NO BUTT! YOU'RE GETTING SMALLER.
NO, I'M NOT. YOU'RE GETTING BIGGER. LOOK DOWN.
IVY, CHECK YOURSELF.
YOU'RE GETTING YOUNGER.
OH GOD.
WHOA, SHIII...!
DILLON!

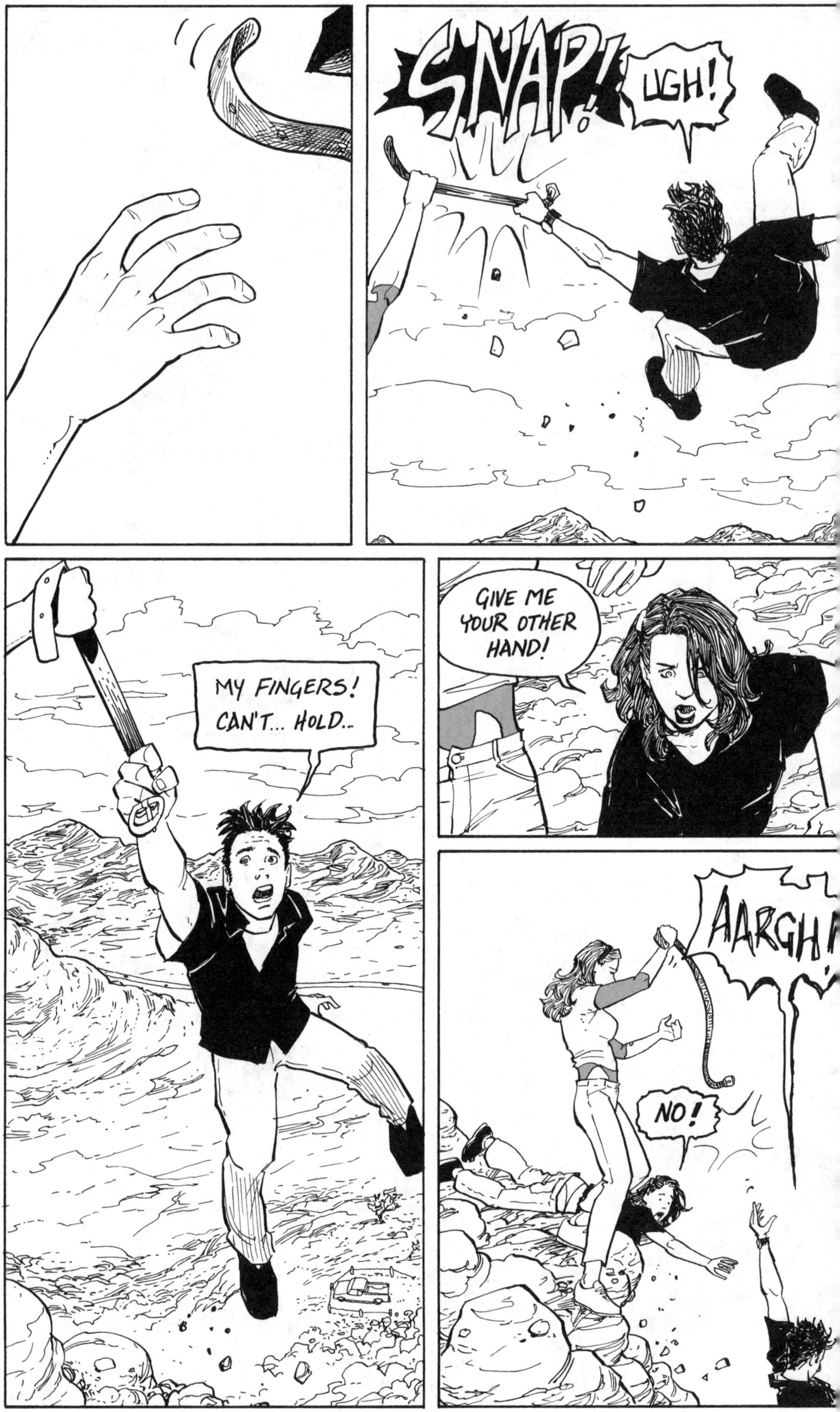
SNAP!
UGH!
MY FINGERS! CAN'T... HOLD..
GIVE ME YOUR OTHER HAND!
AARGH
NO!

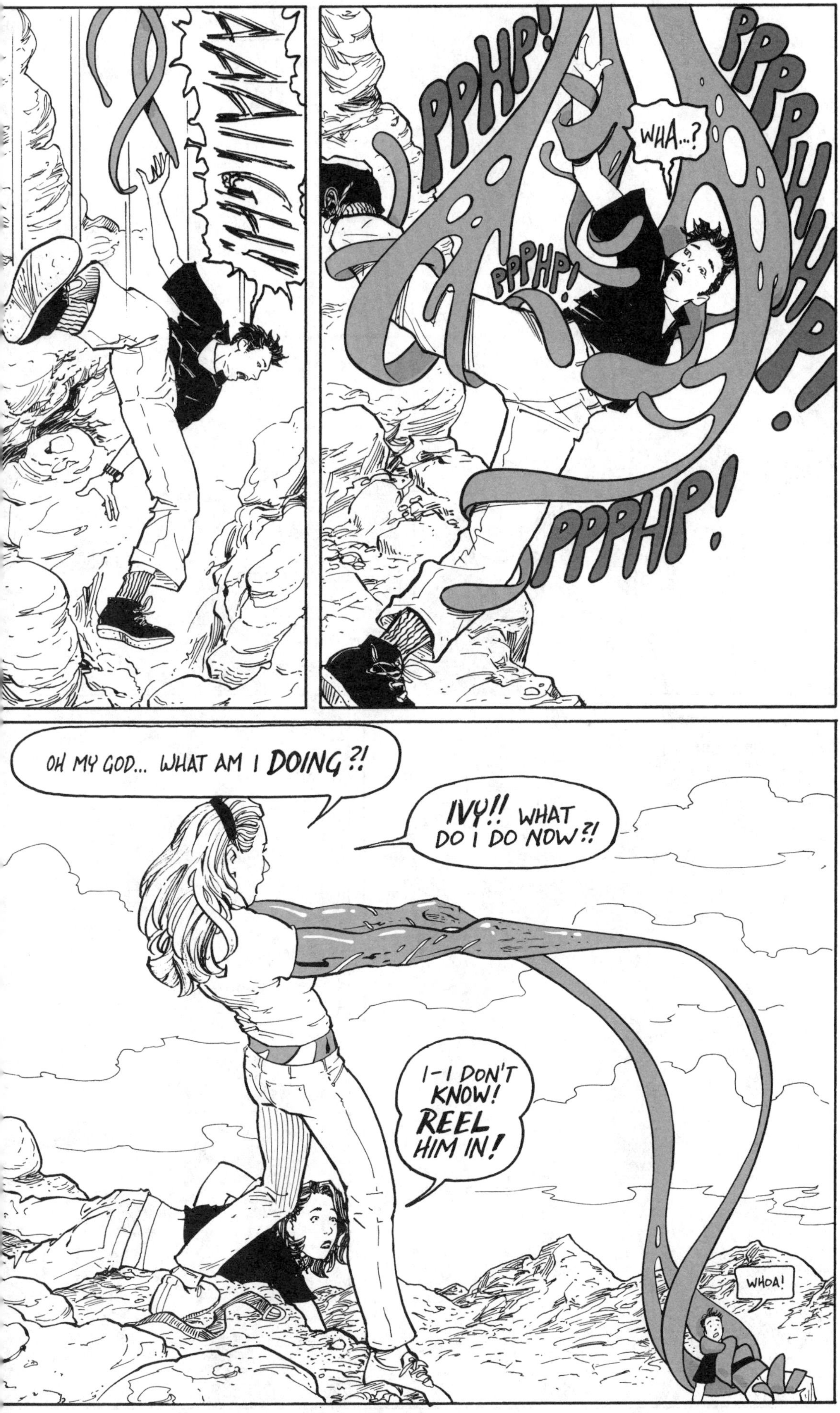
AAAIIGHH!
PPHP!
PPPHP!
WHA...?
PPPRHHP!
PPPHP!
OH MY GOD... WHAT AM I DOING?!
IVY!! WHAT DO I DO NOW?!
I-I DON'T KNOW! REEL HIM IN!
WHOA!

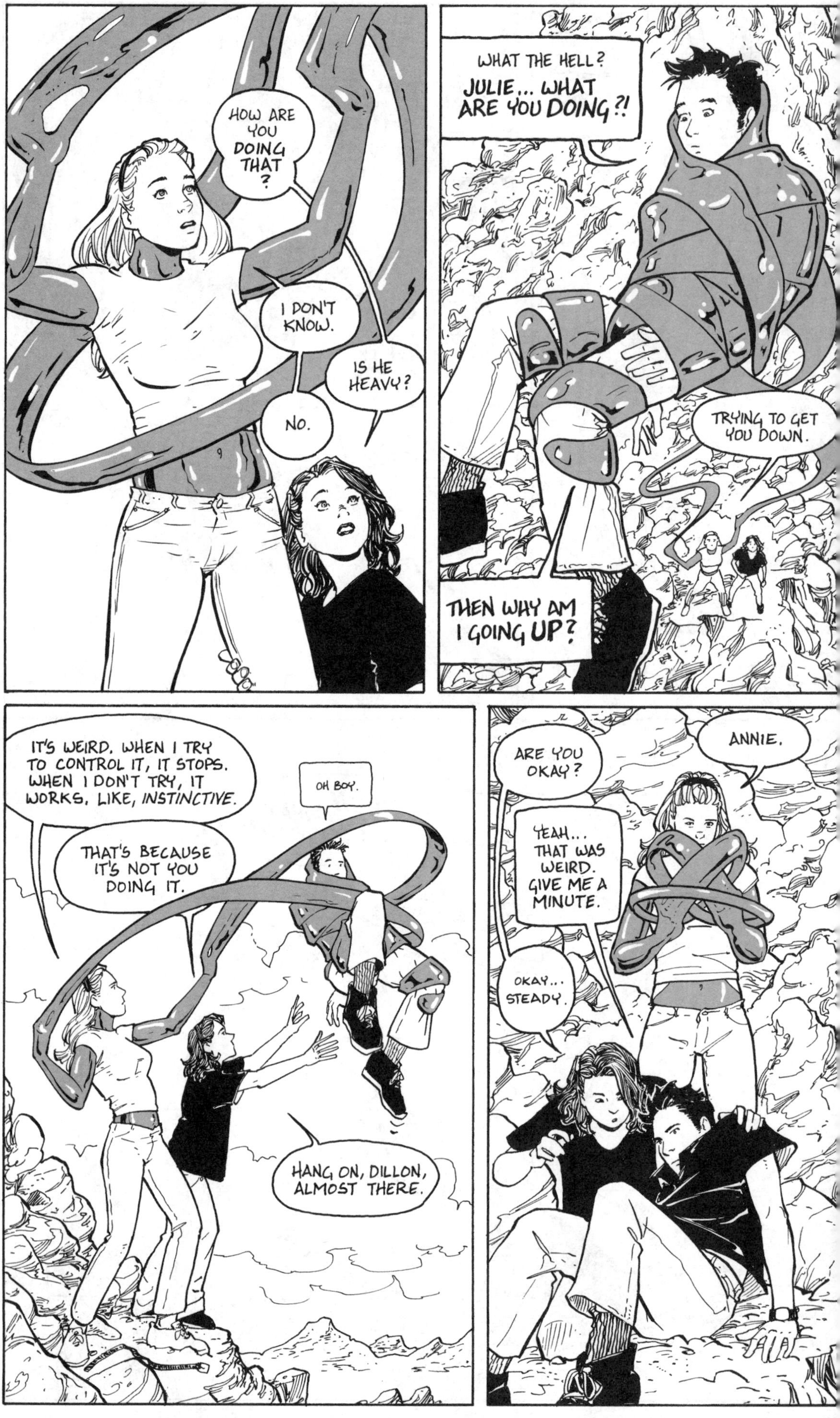
HOW ARE YOU DOING THAT?
I DON'T KNOW.
IS HE HEAVY?
NO.
WHAT THE HELL? JULIE... WHAT ARE YOU DOING?!
TRYING TO GET YOU DOWN.
THEN WHY AM I GOING UP?
IT'S WEIRD. WHEN I TRY TO CONTROL IT, IT STOPS. WHEN I DON'T TRY, IT WORKS. LIKE, INSTINCTIVE.
THAT'S BECAUSE IT'S NOT YOU DOING IT.
OH BOY.
HANG ON, DILLON, ALMOST THERE.
ARE YOU OKAY?
ANNIE.
YEAH... THAT WAS WEIRD. GIVE ME A MINUTE.
OKAY... STEADY.

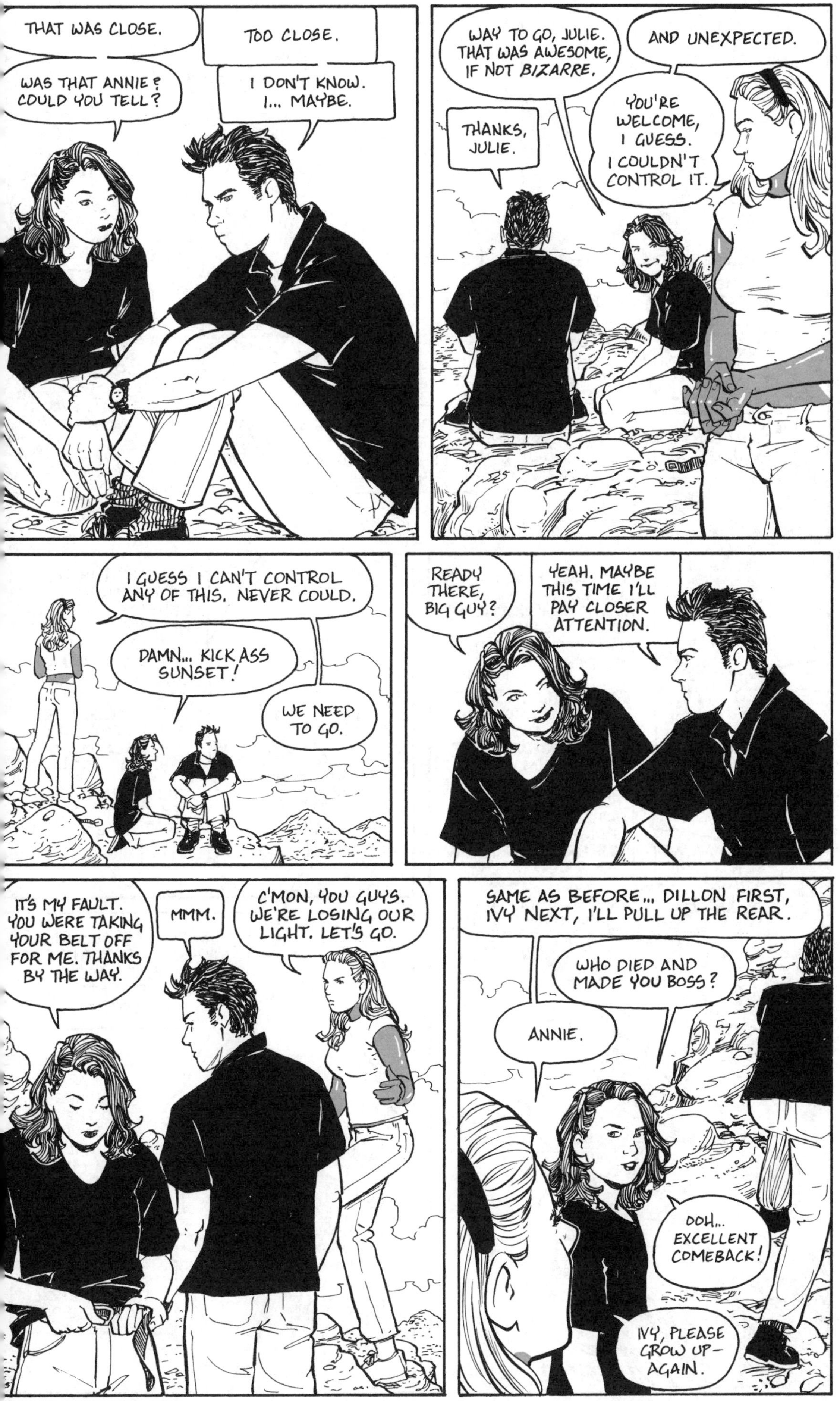
THAT WAS CLOSE.
TOO CLOSE.
WAS THAT ANNIE? COULD YOU TELL?
I DON'T KNOW. I... MAYBE.
WAY TO GO, JULIE. THAT WAS AWESOME, IF NOT BIZARRE.
AND UNEXPECTED.
THANKS, JULIE.
YOU'RE WELCOME, I GUESS. I COULDN'T CONTROL IT.
I GUESS I CAN'T CONTROL ANY OF THIS. NEVER COULD.
DAMN... KICK ASS SUNSET!
WE NEED TO GO.
READY THERE, BIG GUY?
YEAH. MAYBE THIS TIME I'LL PAY CLOSER ATTENTION.
IT'S MY FAULT. YOU WERE TAKING YOUR BELT OFF FOR ME. THANKS BY THE WAY.
MMM.
C'MON, YOU GUYS. WE'RE LOSING OUR LIGHT. LET'S GO.
SAME AS BEFORE... DILLON FIRST, IVY NEXT, I'LL PULL UP THE REAR.
WHO DIED AND MADE YOU BOSS?
ANNIE.
OOH... EXCELLENT COMEBACK!
IVY, PLEASE GROW UP— AGAIN.

THE TIME IS AT HAND,...
THE PROPHECY FULFILLED.

DEATH COMES AT LAST,
DISGUISED AS A CHILD.

EVEN SO, COME QUICKLY,
AZRAEL. I AM WEARY OF
LIFE, AND DEATH ADORNS
YOU LIKE A SMILE.

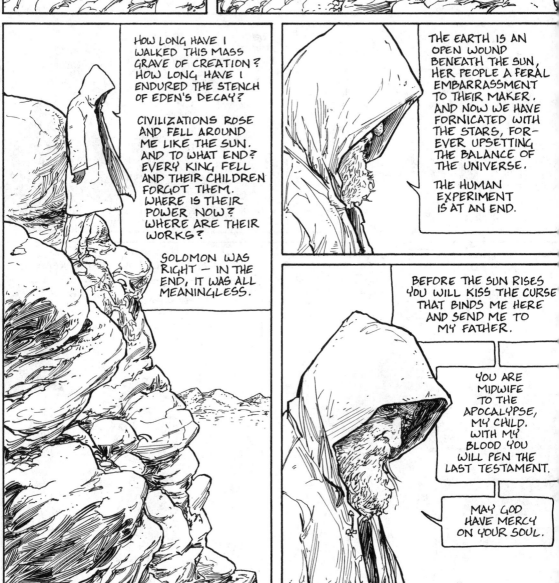

HOW LONG HAVE I
WALKED THIS MASS
GRAVE OF CREATION?
HOW LONG HAVE I
ENDURED THE STENCH
OF EDEN'S DECAY?

CIVILIZATIONS ROSE
AND FELL AROUND
ME LIKE THE SUN.
AND TO WHAT END?
EVERY KING FELL
AND THEIR CHILDREN
FORGOT THEM.
WHERE IS THEIR
POWER NOW?
WHERE ARE THEIR
WORKS?

SOLOMON WAS
RIGHT — IN THE
END, IT WAS ALL
MEANINGLESS.

THE EARTH IS AN
OPEN WOUND
BENEATH THE SUN,
HER PEOPLE A FERAL
EMBARRASSMENT
TO THEIR MAKER.
AND NOW WE HAVE
FORNICATED WITH
THE STARS, FOR-
EVER UPSETTING
THE BALANCE OF
THE UNIVERSE.

THE HUMAN
EXPERIMENT
IS AT AN END.

BEFORE THE SUN RISES
YOU WILL KISS THE CURSE
THAT BINDS ME HERE
AND SEND ME TO
MY FATHER.

YOU ARE
MIDWIFE
TO THE
APOCALYPSE,
MY CHILD.
WITH MY
BLOOD YOU
WILL PEN THE
LAST TESTAMENT.

MAY GOD
HAVE MERCY
ON YOUR SOUL.

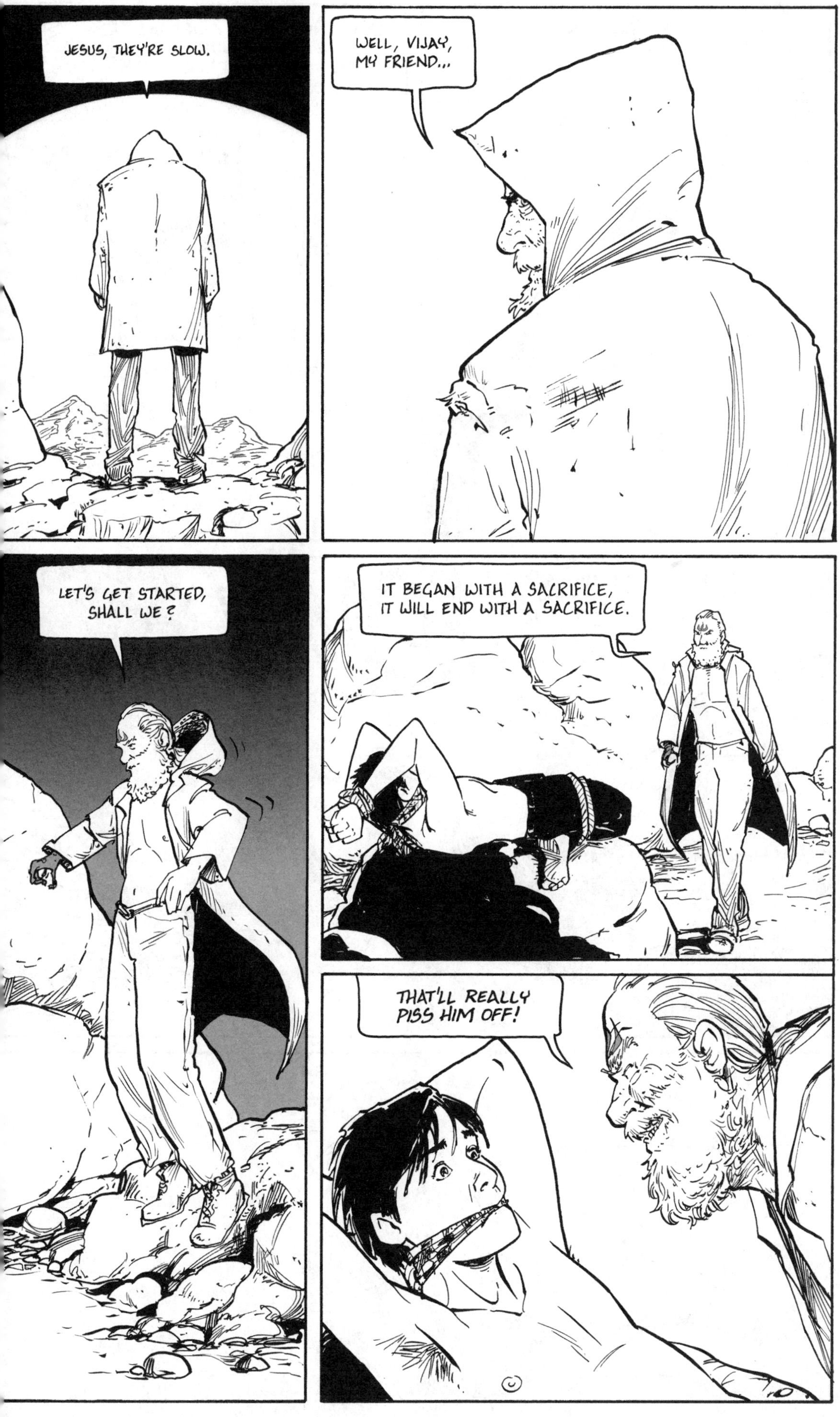
JESUS, THEY'RE SLOW.
WELL, VIJAY, MY FRIEND...
LET'S GET STARTED, SHALL WE?
IT BEGAN WITH A SACRIFICE, IT WILL END WITH A SACRIFICE.
THAT'LL REALLY PISS HIM OFF!

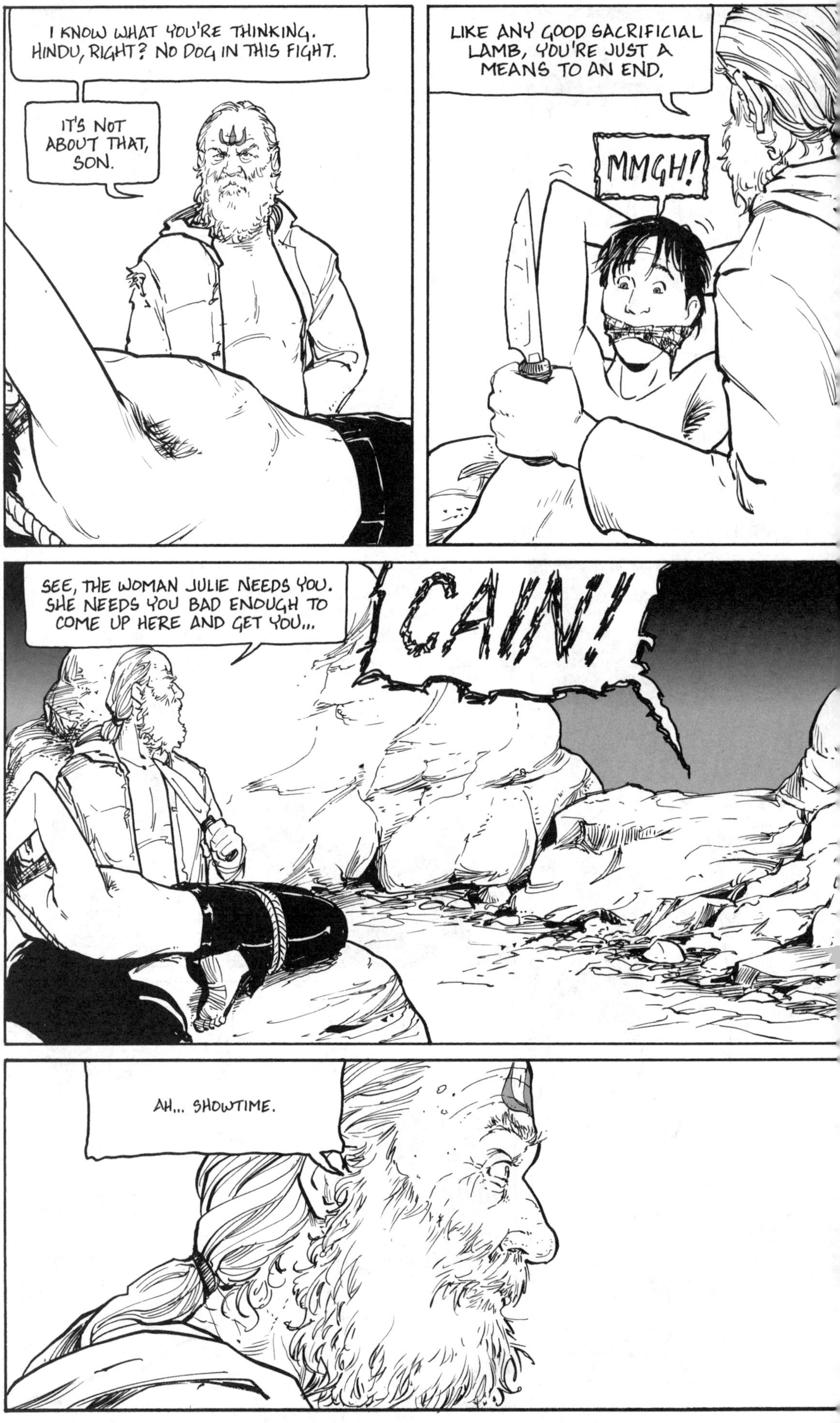
I KNOW WHAT YOU'RE THINKING. HINDU, RIGHT? NO DOG IN THIS FIGHT.
IT'S NOT ABOUT THAT, SON.
LIKE ANY GOOD SACRIFICIAL LAMB, YOU'RE JUST A MEANS TO AN END.
MMGH!
SEE, THE WOMAN JULIE NEEDS YOU. SHE NEEDS YOU BAD ENOUGH TO COME UP HERE AND GET YOU...
CAIN!
AH... SHOWTIME.

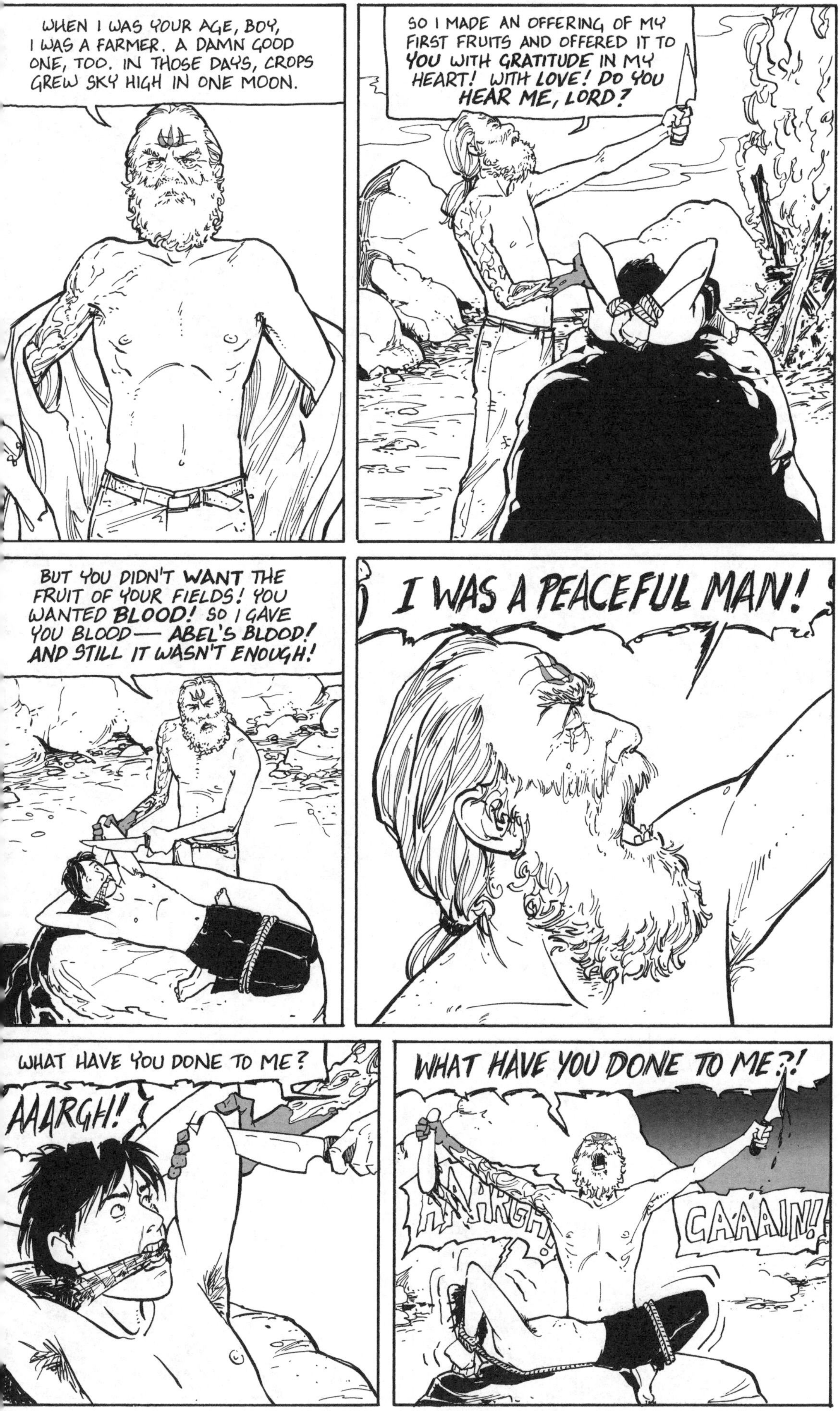
WHEN I WAS YOUR AGE, BOY, I WAS A FARMER. A DAMN GOOD ONE, TOO. IN THOSE DAYS, CROPS GREW SKY HIGH IN ONE MOON.
SO I MADE AN OFFERING OF MY FIRST FRUITS AND OFFERED IT TO YOU WITH GRATITUDE IN MY HEART! WITH LOVE! DO YOU HEAR ME, LORD?
BUT YOU DIDN'T WANT THE FRUIT OF YOUR FIELDS! YOU WANTED BLOOD! SO I GAVE YOU BLOOD— ABEL'S BLOOD! AND STILL IT WASN'T ENOUGH!
I WAS A PEACEFUL MAN!
WHAT HAVE YOU DONE TO ME?
AAARGH!
WHAT HAVE YOU DONE TO ME?!
AAARGH!
CAAAIN!

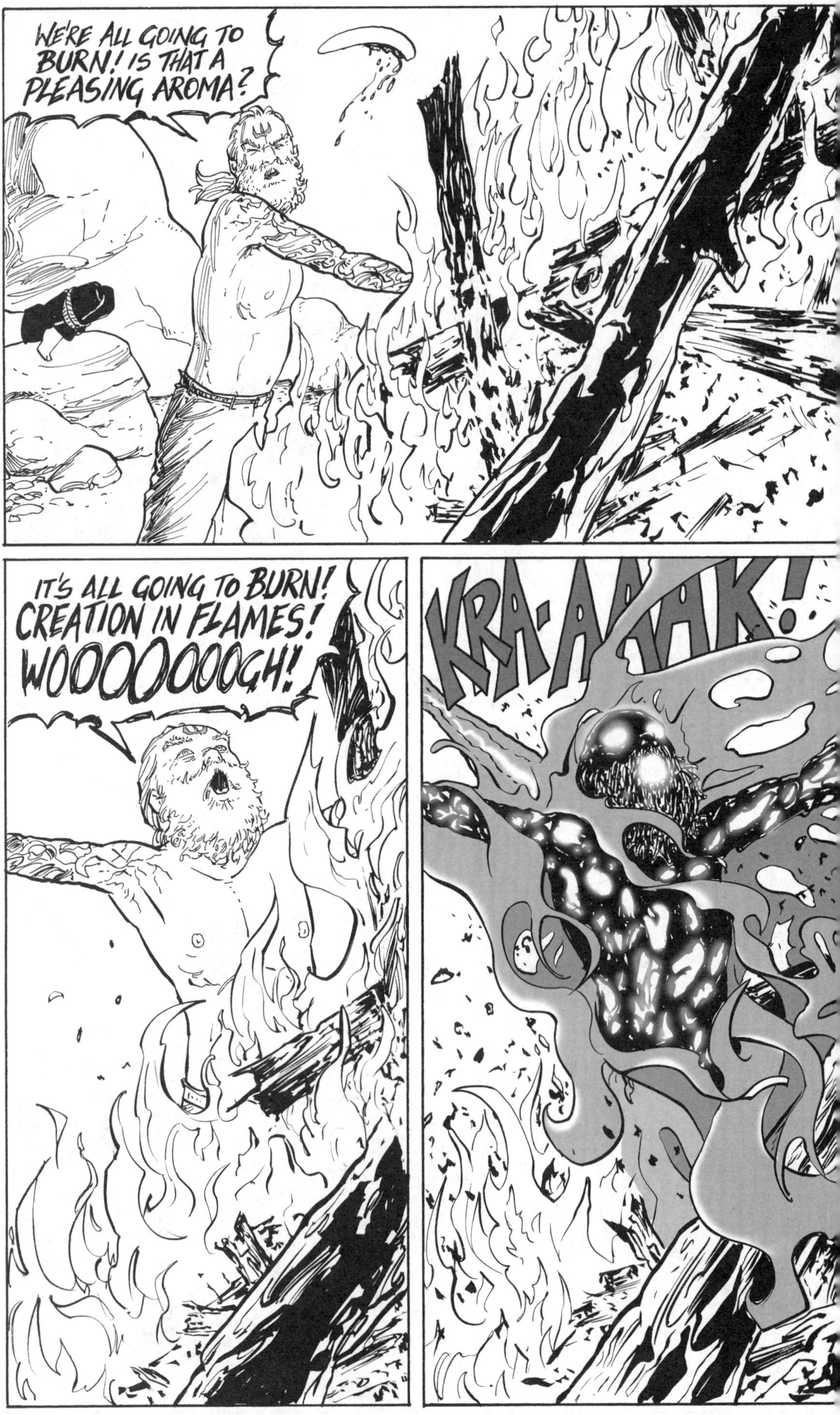
WE'RE ALL GOING TO BURN! IS THAT A PLEASING AROMA?
IT'S ALL GOING TO BURN! CREATION IN FLAMES! WOOOOOOOOGH!
KRA-AAAK!

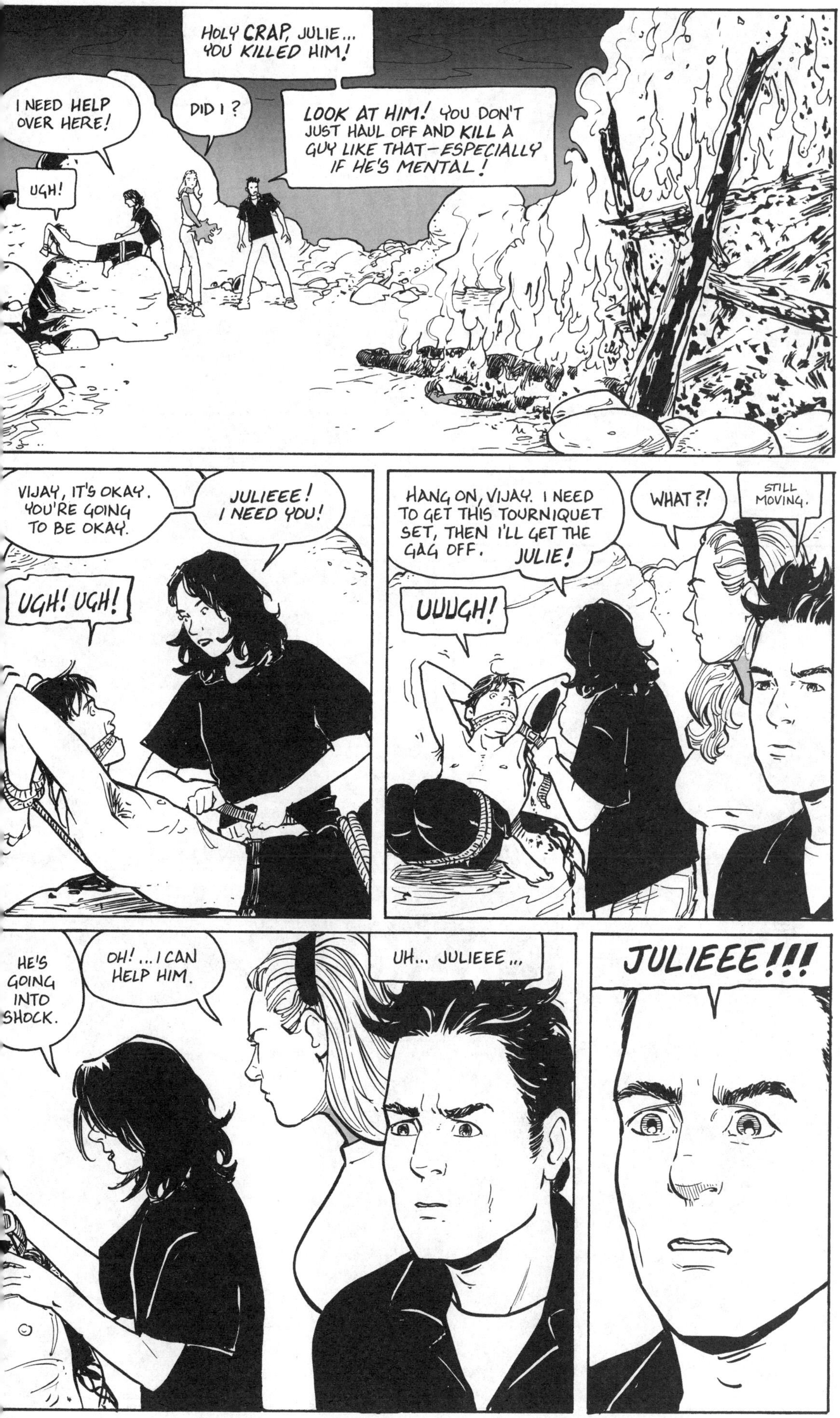
HOLY CRAP, JULIE... YOU KILLED HIM!
I NEED HELP OVER HERE!
DID I?
LOOK AT HIM! YOU DON'T JUST HAUL OFF AND KILL A GUY LIKE THAT—ESPECIALLY IF HE'S MENTAL!
UGH!
VIJAY, IT'S OKAY. YOU'RE GOING TO BE OKAY.
JULIEEE! I NEED YOU!
UGH! UGH!
HANG ON, VIJAY. I NEED TO GET THIS TOURNIQUET SET, THEN I'LL GET THE GAG OFF.
WHAT?!
STILL MOVING.
JULIE!
UUUGH!
HE'S GOING INTO SHOCK.
OH! ...I CAN HELP HIM.
UH... JULIEEE...
JULIEEE!!!

HA! HA! HA!

WAIT!

STAY BACK, DILLON.

YOU CAN'T HURT ME! I'M IMMORTAL!

I DON'T CARE. ALL I WANT IS...

...THIS!

KRA-AAK!

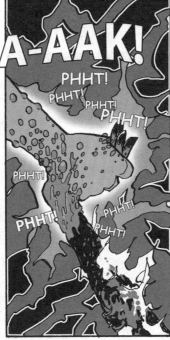

PHHT!
PHHT!
PHHT!
PHHT!

PHHT!

PHHT!
PHHT!

AAAAGH!!

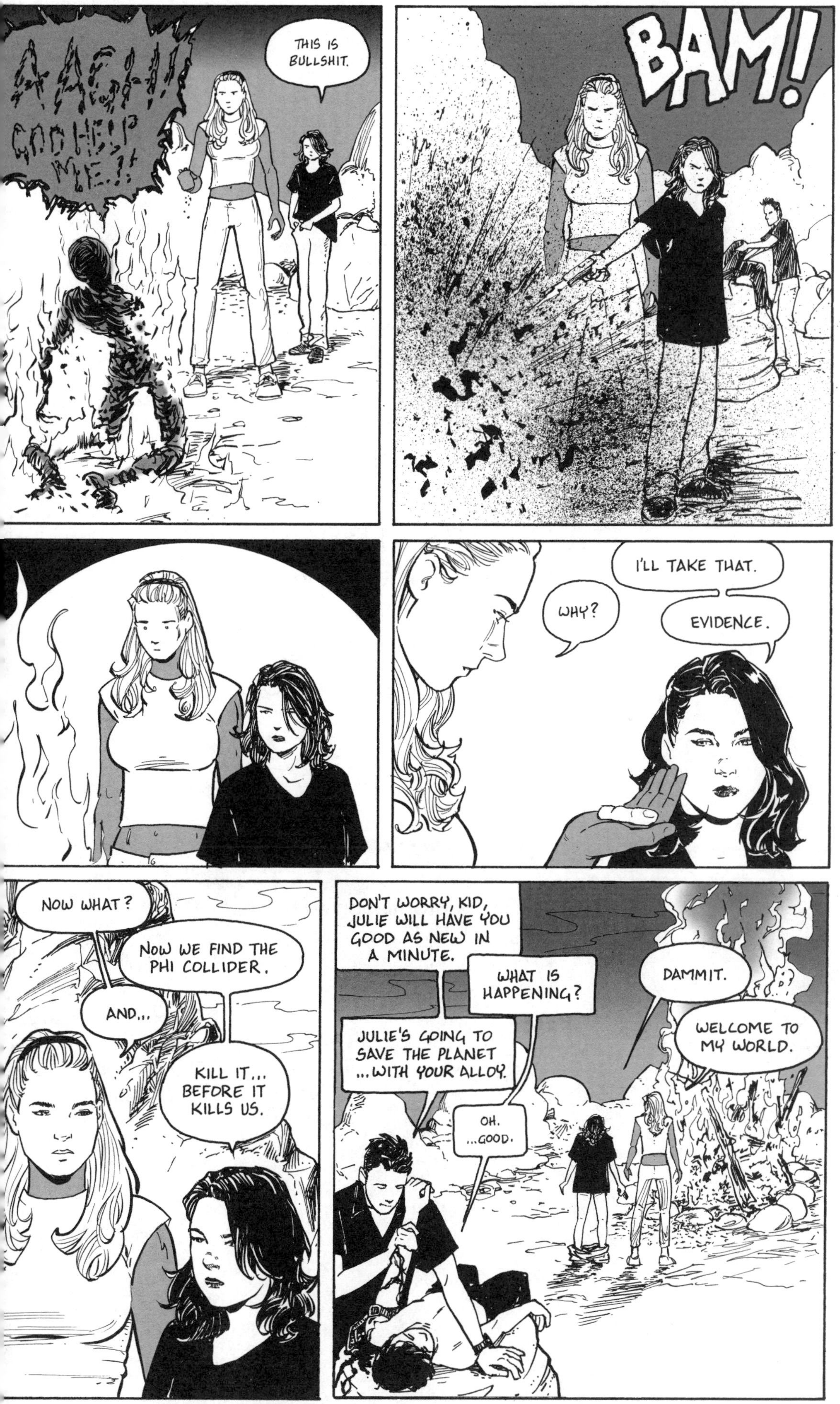
AAGH!! GOD HELP ME!!
THIS IS BULLSHIT.
BAM!
WHY?
I'LL TAKE THAT.
EVIDENCE.
NOW WHAT?
NOW WE FIND THE PHI COLLIDER.
AND...
KILL IT... BEFORE IT KILLS US.
DON'T WORRY, KID, JULIE WILL HAVE YOU GOOD AS NEW IN A MINUTE.
WHAT IS HAPPENING?
JULIE'S GOING TO SAVE THE PLANET ...WITH YOUR ALLOY.
OH. ...GOOD.
DAMMIT.
WELCOME TO MY WORLD.

Books by Terry Moore

ECHO
Moon Lake
Atomic Dreams
Desert Run
Collider

STRANGERS IN PARADISE
Pocket Editions 1 - 6

PARADISE TOO
The Collected Paradise TOO

For more information go to
abstractstudiocomics.com